THE BUTCHER, THE BAKER,
THE WINE & CHEESE MAKER
IN THE OKANAGAN

JENNIFER SCHELL

THE BUTCHER, THE BAKER, THE WINE & CHEESE MAKER

IN THE OKANAGAN

TouchWood
Editions

COVER CAST

BACK ROW (FROM LEFT TO RIGHT): Sandrine Martin-Raffault (pastry and chocolate maker), Lisa Dueck (chicken farmer) with Javier the Wonder Chicken (chicken extraordinaire), Judie Barta (farmer, beekeeper, and honey winemaker), Geoffrey Couper (chef), Jon Alcock (farmer), Howard Soon (winemaker), Gavin Miller (winemaker).

FRONT ROW (FROM LEFT TO RIGHT): Jennifer Schell (author), Sara Harker (farmer, cider and fruit winemaker), Shana Miller (cheese maker), David Paterson (winemaker) with Ella (winery dog and chicken lover).

BRITISH COLUMBIA
Vancouver

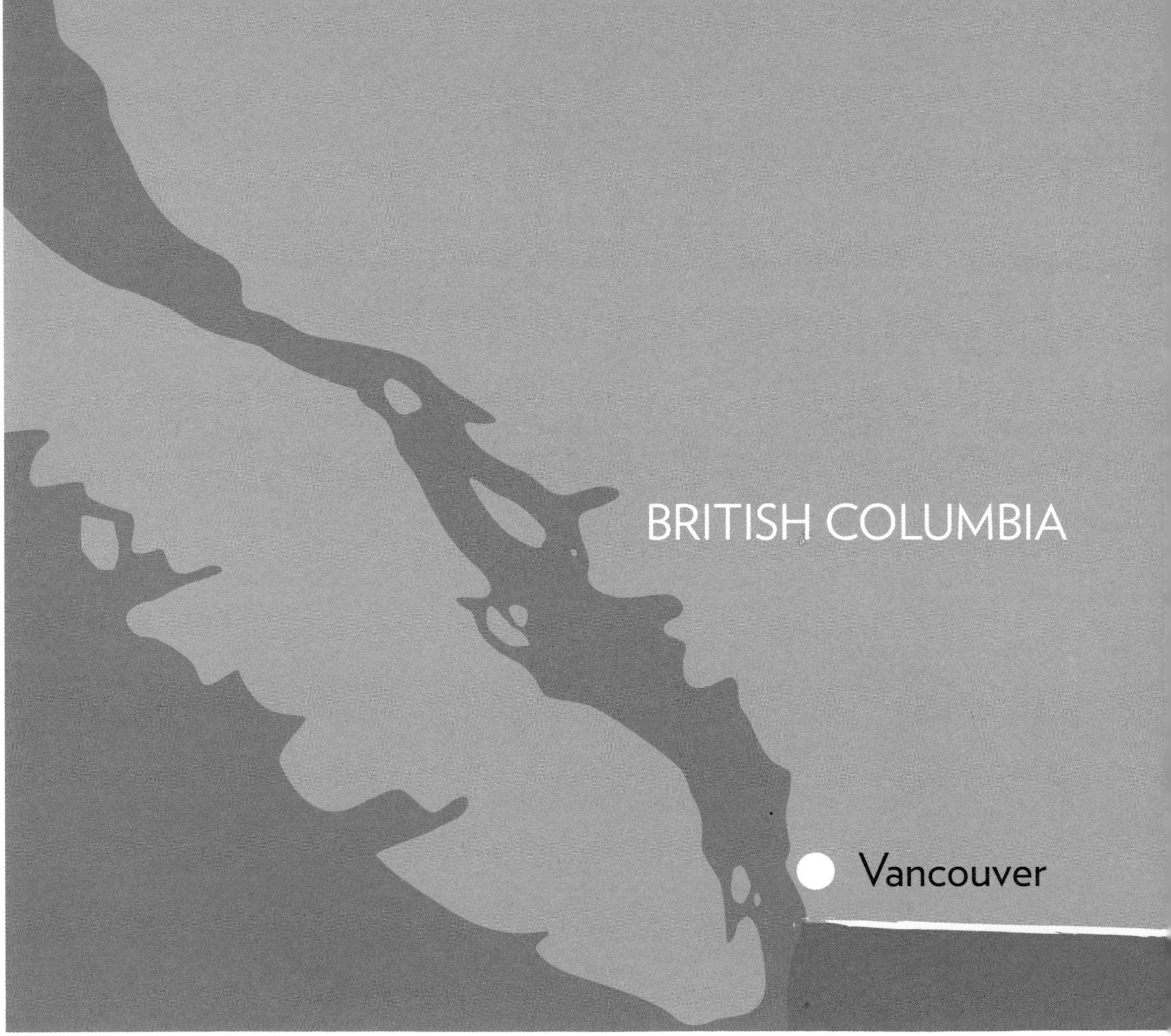

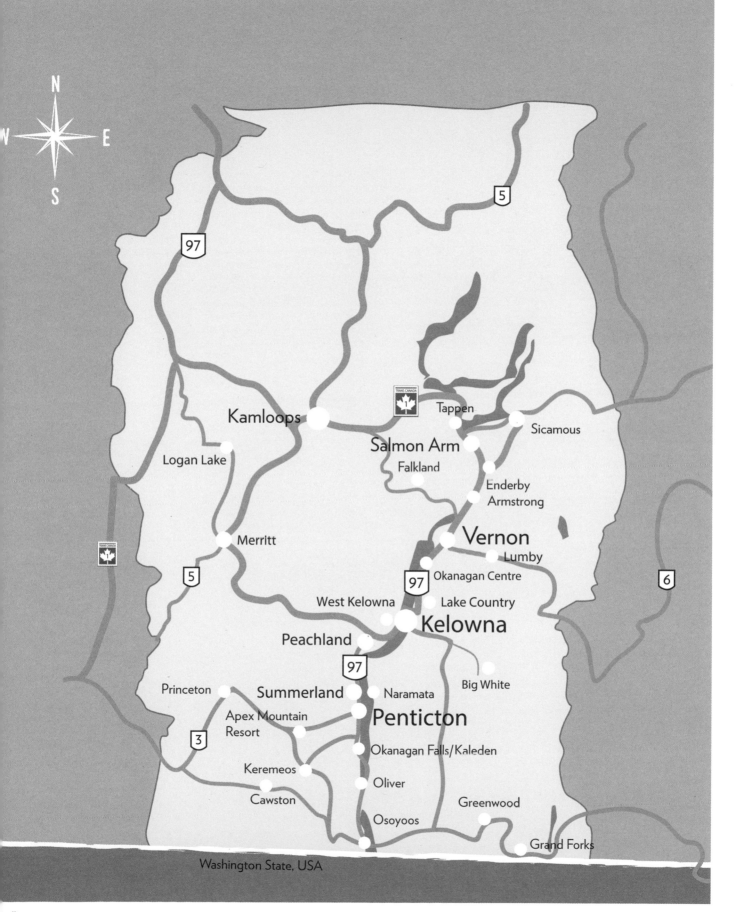

Designer: Pete Kohut
Editor: Claire Philipson

LIBRARY AND ARCHIVES CANADA CATALOGUING IN PUBLISHING
Schell, Jennifer, 1968–, author
The butcher, the baker, the wine & cheese maker in the okanagan / Jennifer Schell.

Issued in print and electronic formats.
ISBN 978-1-77151-156-8

1. Cooking, Canadian—British Columbia style. 2. Cooking—British Columbia—Okanagan Valley (Region). 3. Food—British Columbia—Okanagan Valley (Region). 4. Cookbooks I. Title.

TX715.6.S2694 2016   641.59711′5   C2015-907625-0

We acknowledge the financial support of the Government of Canada through the Canada Book Fund.

Funded by the Government of Canada | Canadä

This book was produced using FSC®-certified, acid-free papers, processed chlorine free, and printed with vegetable-based inks.

PRINTED IN CANADA AT FRIESENS

16 17 18 19 20   5 4 3 2 1

To the farmers, chefs, artisans, winemakers, foragers, fishers, and drinkmakers of the Okanagan and Similkameen Valley. Thank you for feeding us.

CONTENTS

Introduction

I was farm raised on this beautiful Okanagan soil. Proud. I am proud of my family's farming history, with generations of farmers on both sides. I was instilled with a deep respect for the good earth and for those who tend it. My 98-year-old grandma, Katherine Weisbeck, recounts stories of me hopping through the orchard, pigtails flying, with a fistful of wild violets (or whatever I could forage) en route for a visit. She was a fabulous baker and I would love to take my seat—on a large flour tin stacked onto a chair—and watch her bake. She raised eight children on that farm, so her garden and kitchen production levels were a marvel to observe.

My dad's parents, Oma and Opa (Julianna and Lambert) Schell, lived on the other side of our farm until they retired. Their kitchen was another delicious culinary destination for me as a child. Oma's chicken noodle soup remains the best I have ever had. Chock-full of long, homemade egg noodles and rich farm chicken broth—it is a wonderful sensory memory. Soup and homemade sweet milk buns were followed by a slice of her legendary *Zucker Kuchen* (a German-Russian dessert). My palate was honed on homemade, homegrown, made-from-scratch cuisine—and the bar was set high. I was so fortunate to grow up with grandparents living on farms on either side of our own.

When he was eight years old, my dad, John Schell, immigrated from Germany to Canada in 1950 with his family. They had nothing in their pockets but a transport bill of two thousand dollars in their pocket. Sponsored by a distant relative, who owned a restaurant called the Schell Grill on Bernard Avenue in Kelowna, the family first worked for him to pay off their debt before getting numerous jobs around town. A family of five, they worked together—first to survive and eventually to make a good living. After only four years, in the fall of 1954, through hard work and focus, they were able to purchase their own orchard in East Kelowna in the fall of 1954—an extraordinary feat. The harvest time in the 1950s was a crucial period for my family and entailed much more than a fruit harvest. Dad says after they got the fruit off the trees and to the packing house and cannery, it was time to press the grapes for wine (using Opa's handmade grape press), get the potatoes and hearty vegetables into cellar storage, and preserve the fruits and vegetables. Once those chores were complete, when the weather cooled in November, they would butcher pigs and make sausage. Today, we call it sustainability; they called it survival. Then it was time for a celebration dinner, usually a pig roast. The wine flowed, the table was laden with their hard-earned bounty, and they would share the feast with friends and family and raise their glasses to life.

It is amazing to imagine that their family was almost completely self-sufficient—from produce to meat to dairy products to wine to soap. Opa's deep respect for his land, knowledge of how to grow food, raise food, and create from the earth is the foundation of our food and wine culture here. This life-giving soil gave them everything they needed to survive, and so it remains for us. This cookbook is a love letter to all those who have created, grown, and nurtured our special valley on this earth. They are a delightful confluence of old and new world, blending their international influence and flavours with our local bounty, establishing a cuisine that is distinctly Okanagan. Through their recipes and stories, I am pleased to introduce you to these gifted people who bring this local food to your table every day.

A new generation is choosing farming because they want to tend the soil, support community, and be able to feed their families. So help me cheer each and every one of these young agrarians on. I will introduce you to them here, and hope you will make a point to meet them and purchase their produce to help them grow.

JENNIFER SCHELL

Foreword by Mark Filatow

Coming from Vancouver and Vancouver Island, I have seen, cooked, and tasted the wares of some really good farmers and fishmongers. One of my favourite farmers came over to the West Coast from the Okanagan once a week with tomatoes that were akin to candy. Now he jokes that my backyard versions are competing with his.

In this cookbook, Jennifer has amassed a clutch of people who are like-minded in their search of and contribution to a sustainable local food and wine scene.

I moved to the Okanagan in 2001. The produce, the climate, the wines, the outdoors all dragged me here. What a great place to be a chef who loves wine—and what was a good selection of farms and wineries then has now exploded!

The supply has changed. The farmers' markets have changed. The markets have grown in popularity, size, and offerings. The sheer number of farms astounds me. Things that weren't widely available then are now: organic pork, fresh chicken, free-range lamb, freshly milled flours, apple varieties long forgotten, elderflower honey, local spirits, and storage crops available deep into winter. At the restaurant we have a local potato supply until May. That's ten months a year!

Young farmers and producers are springing up everywhere, and are bringing their families with them. This succession helps me realize the full potential of what we have here, and gives me hope for the future.

I am the benefactor of this and so are you. So are my workmates, patrons of the farms and restaurants that have recipes in this book, and my family. One night, while having a dinner at home, my nine-year-old daughter looked up from her plate and exclaimed, "This is the best piece of meat I have ever eaten." It was a Wild Moon Organic Berkshire pork loin. I looked at her, nodded in agreement, and watched her take a forkful of carrot grown in our own backyard. Knowing that she will forever compare everything she will taste to that memory made me smile.

Having travelled to various parts of the world to experience food and wine, I know that the produce and the wine made here stands head-to-head with the global output. In many cases it even stands taller. Tomatoes are the benchmark that I use to make this statement. But we grow many things other than great tomatoes!

Thank you to the farmers and producers that are keeping me from going hungry and thirsty.

Thank you, Jennifer, for putting these ideas in print, and for reminding us to look no further than our own backyard.

Foreword by Jon Alcock

Jennifer's *Butcher, Baker, Wine & Cheese Maker* series is not simply a series of cookbooks. It is an exposition of an important cultural phenomenon; it helps put the culture back into agriculture; it is a cog in the gear of supporting local economies; it embodies the idea of "coming home to eat," and reveres our land for what it is: that which sustains and inspires us.

I have seen the Okanagan transformed from forest to farm to orchard to vineyard to golf course and housing development. Agriculture is such an important element of our landscape and our mindscape. It reminds us of a time when all our food came from the land on which we live, when there were no fences, no rows of vegetables or fruit trees, no agrochemicals. A time when we lived in harmony with the earth and harvested our foods in a sustainable manner from forest, field, and stream. Growing up in Kelowna, I had the good fortune to live close to this ancient harmony. Gathering asparagus from alongside the irrigation ditches, pulling brook and rainbow trout from the streams, and hunting grouse and deer from the forest and mushrooms from the field were important parts of our family sustenance.

As a student at the University of Victoria doing cross-cultural analysis on now-antiquated microfiche files, I studied subsistence strategies around the world and realized how important farming was to human existence and evolution. At a time when farming and local food production were on the decline in the Western world, and exotic, imported food in a supermarket was the new paradigm, swimming against the current was a noble cause for me. That meant sustainable, regenerative agriculture, as historically practiced by indigenous people around the world. It was a lofty goal in a culture that wantonly tossed around petroleum as pesticides, fuels, and fertilizers. We started farming in a time when there were no quick alternatives to agrochemicals, so

we needed to develop strategies on our own scale that optimized sustainable methods: composting, green manures, rotations, beneficial insects, scheduled planting around the life cycles of insects, and building our soils rather than depleting them. Ultimately, working with the earth's natural systems and not against them.

One of the reasons organic food production and consumption, especially in North America, continues to grow at 20 percent per year is that the flavour profiles of organic food are so much better than industrially grown food. Organically grown carrots, tomatoes, strawberries, and apples are the best indicators of this, likely due to the higher levels of antioxidants and lower levels of nitrates.

According to the UN Food and Agriculture Organization, more than 80 percent of the world's food production comes from small family farms. In fact, it forecasts that the small organic family farm will be the only way to sustainably feed the human population in years to come. It is our hope that we will see a return to this type of agriculture in the industrialized world. Obviously this will require a huge shift to more sustainable methods, a shift to support local food production and local economies. Think of Detroit. As it loses its industry and population, it is returning to the farmland and forest it was when Algonquin-speaking peoples grew corn, beans, and squash and foraged from the surrounding forest. Land is being remediated and is providing "green groceries" where previously only convenience store "food" was available.

The premise of Jennifer's book is brilliant. It allows all the players to illustrate the mutual respect we have for one another and how, in this small pocket of Canada, we can live well, embracing all our cultures through food as a microcosm of what we hope for the future of the planet.

BRUNCHIE LUNCHIE

The Curious Eggs Benny

This is one of the most delicious bennies around. The spicy harissa sauce adds the perfect morning kick and the made-from-scratch English muffins make you look like a rock star. The Curious Café—and the other Kelowna eateries in Luigi Coccaro's restaurant empire—uses Soil Mate as its go-to tool to source the best local ingredients.

Serves 6

Enjoy with 2013 Ava, Le Vieux Pin Winery
A bold and enticing wine with subtle undertones of lemon.

In a pot, warm milk and butter to 110°F (43°C). Sift flour into a large mixing bowl. Look at the bowl as though it was a clock; pour the yeast into the bowl at 12 o'clock, the sugar at 4 o'clock, and the salt at 7 o'clock.

Whisk the eggs to break up the yolks and, using a spatula, begin mixing the eggs into the bowl of flour. Follow with warmed milk and butter.

Once the mixture becomes dough, pour onto a clean surface and knead gently for 5 minutes. Cover the dough with a clean, lightly moistened cloth and place in a warm area to proof.

Once the dough has risen to double its size, roll out with a rolling pin to ¾-inch (2-cm) thick. Cut rounds with a 2-inch diameter circular cookie cutter.

Let rise once more.

Heat up a non-stick pan or an electric griddle to medium heat. Dust lightly with cornmeal and place English muffins inside.

Once golden, flip and repeat.

When the muffins are golden on both sides, place in oven at 375°F (190°C) until the sides of the muffin set. Cool.

Harissa hot sauce: Sweat onions, shallots, and garlic in a few tablespoons of grapeseed oil in a medium saucepot over medium heat. Add white pepper, coriander, caraway, and dried peppers until fragrant. Add red peppers and cook until soft. Add tomato paste and paprika and cook slowly until very dry. Add vinegar and stock and simmer for 20 minutes. Pour mixture into a blender, add mint leaves and carefully blend until smooth. Pour through a fine strainer and cool. Adjust seasoning with white pepper, salt, and sugar.

To serve: Cut muffins in half and place poached egg atop each cut side. Top with harissa hot sauce and serve with a side of hash browns. Enjoy!

English muffins
Makes 12 muffins

12 fl oz (360 mL) homogenized milk

2 Tbsp (30 mL) butter

2½ cups (625 mL) all-purpose flour

2½ tsp (12 mL) instant yeast

2 Tbsp (30 mL) sugar

2½ tsp (12 mL) salt

2 eggs

cornmeal for dusting

Harissa hot sauce
2 small white onions, diced

2 small shallots, diced

4 small cloves garlic, diced

3–4 Tbsp (45–60 mL) grapeseed oil

1 Tbsp (15 mL) white pepper

3 Tbsp (45 mL) coriander seed, ground

2 Tbsp (30 mL) caraway seeds

1 gaujillo pepper, dried

3 arbol peppers, dried

2 Tbsp (30 mL) chili flakes, dried

6 small red bell peppers, diced

¼ cup (75 mL) tomato paste

3 Tbsp (45 mL) paprika

¼ cup (75 mL) sherry vinegar

3 cups (750 mL) vegetable stock

¼ cup (75 mL) mint leaves

white pepper, salt, and sugar to taste

This experience showed me early on where my passions lie."

Chris and his new bride, local chef Evelynn Braun (née Takoff), have a delicious love story that, of course, began in a kitchen. "While working at the Capri Hotel, my chef told me she was hiring the daughter of a family friend and that I was to teach her to cook. I remember her saying, 'She doesn't know how to hold a knife yet,' and being fairly upset that she was hiring help that was so green! Eventually Evelynn moved on, landing at RauDZ Regional Table where she grew quickly to become Rod Butters' sous chef. Years went by and we began dating. We were married on September 27, 2015, with our son, Sebastian, walking our bridesmaid down the aisle." Chris Braun can now be found behind the pans at micro bar • bites in Kelowna.

f /thecuriouskelowna   thecurious.ca

The Restaurant Maker ✤ Luigi Coccaro
The Curious Café, Kelowna

La Bussola, the Coccaro family's flagship restaurant, has remained one of Kelowna's favourite dining experiences since 1974. Luigi Coccaro's parents, Franco and Loretta, created a menu that reflects their Italian heritage with a foundation of good food and wine—a passion that they passed on to their son.

Luigi's newest endeavour, The Curious Café, graduated him to successful restaurateur in his own right. He is the creative mind behind the concept: a restaurant with a dual personality. It's a café on one side and a pizzeria/tavern-style eatery on the other. New to the restaurant family is the back-room style cocktail lounge, Bar Norcino, that is currently open weekends only; ask the bartender at The Curious for directions.

Luigi has become an integral part of downtown Kelowna's urban growth. The Curious provided its neighbourhood with an immediate shot of vitality and youth, and the addition of a back room space and a new off-site café will continue to drive progress. Luigi

LEFT TO RIGHT: CHRIS BRAUN, LUIGI COCCARO, MATT GOMEZ.

The Chef ✤ Chris Braun
The Curious Café, Kelowna

Chris loves the Okanagan. He says, "This is one of the few cities where all of the chefs are cheering each other on. It is a community of chefs working together to promote one of Canada's richest culinary communities."

Chef at the Curious Café from opening day, Chris Braun was destined for chefdom; his oma (grandmother) spotted it as a child. "I grew up spending my weekends cooking in her kitchen. She taught me basic classic European recipes that she learned from her mother and her oma growing up in Germany.

says, "I love downtown Kelowna. I live downtown, eat downtown, shop downtown. All my friends joke about me being the Earl of Ellis Street as I work and live in a 100-foot radius. He adds, "My parents are a huge part of my life. They inspire me in many ways—especially when it comes to staying closely connected as a family. A solid work ethic has always been important to them, too, and I am really thankful for that. Having this sentimental attachment, and treating my businesses and staff like family, has resulted in a tremendously strong team."

SEVERINE PINTE

The Farm Connector ❖ Matt Gomez
Soil Mate, Kelowna

The Winemaker ❖ Severine Pinte
Le Vieux Pin Winery, Oliver

Soil Mate is an amazing, modern tool that essentially exists to connect consumers directly with farmers/producers. The online platform and directory helps people easily source local food and drink through the farmers and producers that create and raise local food in their community. It was created by local social media whiz, Matt Gomez, who, after starting his own family, realized the importance of feeding his own children healthy, local food.

Since Soil Mate's inception, Matt has deeply integrated himself into the local farm community, formed relationships in the local food and drink world, and has become somewhat of a locavorian expert. Matt is passionate about his new role, and explains, "It's an honour to work with those that feed us. I love being able to help thank them all with tools to support their businesses. Through Soil Mate we can change the way people think about their food, how they buy their food, how they understand their food, and help farmers."

Winner of the Best Concept in BC 2015 at the Small Business BC Awards, Matt's Soil Mate is just beginning and represents the future of shopping local and supporting your community.

Charming and quaint, Le Vieux Pin Winery is the Okanagan's version of a French winemaking house or, as they describe it, "a winery paying homage to the great personalities and wines of France." The name means old pine, and it is romantically named for the old trees on the estate. Appropriately, the talented winemaker and viticulturist, Severine Pinte, came to Le Vieux Pin in 2010 from France, and has been making magic from soil to bottle as a *vigneron* ever since.

f /levieuxpin 🐦 @levieuxpin levieuxpin.ca

f /findmysoilmate 🐦 @mysoilmate soilmate.com

Bohemian Omelette

 HANS BIRKER

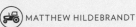 MATTHEW HILDEBRANDT

 ANGELA RITZ

Omelettes seem to be a breakfast item that most people don't make at home. This delightful dish is just the thing to start your day. If you don't feel like cooking, join the mass of happy diners at the Bohemian Café & Catering Company in Kelowna!

Serves 1–2

Enjoy with Ritzy Apple Juice

As pure as can be, this apple juice is just that—100% apples. To ritz it up a bit, add some sparkling water.

Make salad dressing: Whisk all ingredients together vigorously in a bowl and transfer to a jar with a lid for storage. Shake before each use. Set aside. Dressing will keep for a couple weeks in the fridge.

Make omelette right before serving: Whisk together eggs, cream, sea salt, and fresh ground pepper. Set aside.

Rub 4 to 5 slices of zucchini with olive oil and sprinkle with sea salt. Fry until brown on both sides, or add grill marks with a panini machine or a barbecue. If you're barbecuing the night before, make a few extra and refrigerate them for the next morning.

Preheat a 10-inch (25-cm) non-stick frying pan to medium high. Pour in 1 tsp olive oil and swirl around. Pour in the egg mixture. Wait for it to bubble and gently lift the egg wash that's beginning to solidify with a flat silicone spatula. Let the liquid run underneath. Continue this process until no more liquid will flow. Remove from heat. Quickly place the warm zucchini on half the omelette and the Asiago on top of the zucchini. Immediately cover the pan and let stand for 2 minutes. Remove cover and fold the egg half of the omelette over the zucchini and Asiago half.

To serve: Vigorously toss organic wild mixed greens in a large bowl with as much dressing as you like—start with a little and add as you see fit while you're tossing. Remember to always toss well to get the greens evenly dressed.

Slide omelette onto a plate with a nice portion of the dressed organic greens. Loosely scrunch up 2 slices of the prosciutto and place so that it gently drapes off the side of the wild greens. Garnish with a wedge of cantaloupe or honeydew melon.

Salad dressing

2 tsp (10 mL) fresh basil purée (store-bought or make by puréeing fresh basil leaves with olive oil)

2 tsp (10 mL) garlic, minced

1 tsp (5 mL) sea salt

1 tsp (5 mL) black pepper, freshly ground

splash balsamic vinegar

1/3 cup (75 mL) lemon juice

2/3 cup (150 mL) olive oil or grapeseed oil

Omelette

3 free-run eggs

1 Tbsp (15 mL) heavy cream

dash sea salt

2 turns fresh ground pepper

1 medium zucchini, cut into 1/4-inch slices

Olive oil

2 1/4 Tbsp (35 g) Asiago cheese, grated

1 handful per person Morning Dove Gardens wild greens, for serving

2 slices prosciutto, for serving (Buy the best Italian prosciutto and get your butcher to slice it as thinly as possible while still getting a full slice)

wedge honeydew melon or cantaloupe, for garnish

The Restaurant Maker ❖ Hans Birker
The Bohemian Café & Catering Company, Kelowna

Mention "The Boh" to locals in Kelowna and they will inevitably smile (and maybe drool a bit). The Bohemian Café & Catering Company is a local landmark and THE spot for the cool people to breakfast/brunch and generally enjoy good food with friends. The original "Boh" opened further up Bernard Avenue in 1991. Hans Birker and his sister Litti, who both grew up in the food industry, decided to give it a go. And did it go! Immediately after opening their cool new restaurant (at that time it was open all day from 8 AM to 11 PM for three meals), they were a hit. With a creative new menu that tied in family recipes with new food trends (like their legendary turkey curry bagel—back when bagels and curry were a new thing), they were a sensation.

Hans says he and his sister knew it was hard to find jobs here in Kelowna, so they decided to create their own. The family history goes back to Germany, where sausage making was the family trade. Their grandparents had an inn in Uedem, Germany, near Dusseldorf, and that is where his dad learned his art. In 1974 Hans's father brought his family to Canada and built his business, Okanagan Sausage, in Oyama. Ring any bells? Yes, this is the iconic Oyama Sausage family. The legacy continues, now in Vancouver, through the passion of Hans's cousin John van der Lieck, to whom his father sold the business in 1988. Keeping the family's standard of the highest quality and using traditional methods, John and his wife Christine have taken Oyama Sausage to an "elite level," says Hans. The two continue to work together, with Hans featuring some of their products in special event menus.

The current location of The Boh opened in 2005. Hans's wife, Terri, is now a business partner (Litti left the business to pursue other opportunities), and designed the fabulous interior, which is timelessly cool and eclectic. Hans says she was mentally designing that space for 15 years.

The Boh operates a thriving catering business and feeds a packed house of breakfast, brunch, and lunchers each day; many are regulars, and the door usually has a lineup. They have incredible vegetarian and vegan choices as well. When it comes to their philosophy, Hans says, "Our beliefs are simple: start with good quality, local food and turn it into an experience to remember."

f /bohemian-cafe-catering-co-the-boh   bohemiancater.com

The Farmer ❖ Matthew Hildebrandt
Morning Dove Gardens, Kelowna

Morning Dove Gardens is located on a stunning four-acre piece of land near Mission Creek in Kelowna. Rolling green hills, a creek below, and vineyards above—it is picturesque as well as productive. Matthew Hildebrandt and his wife Taryne purchased the property with Matthew's parents. The family shares the gorgeous acreage with Matthew and Taryne's young children, Elias and Mishyla. Before farming, Matthew was a caretaker at a group home, which speaks to his gentle nature. He decided that he wanted to spend more time outside, surrounded by the natural world. He and Taryne also decided that once they started their family they wanted to learn to be self-sufficient and grow their own food. And so they did.

Matthew has farming in his blood; his grandparents on both sides were Dutch Mennonite farmers. "Farming is part of my history," he says. But he also extols the virtues of the new generation of farmers, praising their great passion for the earth and their choice of profession.

One of my favourite things to buy at his stand at the Kelowna Farmer's Market is his wonderful mixed greens, which contain lovely yellow sunflower petals. One day he was picking greens, Matthew tells me, which were planted near a row of decorative sunflowers. He knew that the entire sunflower was edible, so he decided to give them a try.

Currently the farm has two acres planted in garden and a pasture with chicken and goats. Next on the

LEFT TO RIGHT: HANS BIRKER AND MATTHEW HILDEBRANDT

ANGELA RITZ

agenda is to build green houses. Matthew says, "My goal is to have greens available all year 'round." For now, Morning Dove Gardens sells produce at the Kelowna Farmers' Market, offers a CSA (community assisted agriculture) program and also supplies produce to Urban Harvest for its organic basket deliveries (see page 70).

f /morning-dove-gardens   morningdove.ca

The Apple Juice Maker ❖ Angela Ritz
East Kelowna

Angela Ritz (née Stepphun) grew up on the apple orchard behind my family's orchard. Angela and her husband, Frank, now have their own orchard nearby in the Southeast Kelowna orchard district. It is a small farm, producing enough apples to ship some to the local packinghouse with the remainder going to friends and family and into her delicious apple juice. The juice was initially created to use up the culled apples and windfalls (those dropped to the ground); this is a farm girl who knows about sustainability! The juice is made from a blend of her various varieties: McIntosh, Golden Delicious, Aurora Golden Gala, Nicola, Spartans, and Ambrosia. Angela hires the

Okanagan Mobile Juicing truck to come to the farm and vacuum-pack the juice into cartons. This way, the juice lasts on the counter for months and the freshness is sealed in with zero preservatives—it is 100 percent natural apple juice. Cartons of it will be available for sale starting in 2016 at The Boh restaurant.

The Juicers ❖ Kristen & Remo Trovato
Okanagan Mobile Juicing, Vernon

Kirsten and Remo Trovato are the names behind the juicing biz, and they explain: "We have come to learn the struggle that growers in the Okanagan face every year—low prices for fruit, increased prices for services, and no government support, be it from lack of subsidies or refusing to establish anti-dumping tariffs on imported fruit. We hope that by providing an alternative, value-added product for growers, we can also provide a small growth to their income. Hopefully this will result in growers keeping their orchards and continue to grow the fruit that the Okanagan is known for, therefore sustaining our culture, our economy, and our environment."

f /mobilejuicing   🐦 @MobileJuicing   mobilejuicing.com

Short Ribs 'n' Eggs

 JASON LEIZERT

 SARA & TROY HARKER

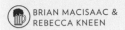 BRIAN MACISAAC & REBECCA KNEEN

Chef Jason Leizart specializes in comfort food. Meals like this served at his Salted Brick restaurant are why he has gained such a dedicated following. This is gourmet soul food—no one leaves the Brick hungry.

Serves 4

Enjoy with Crannóg Ales' Gael's Blood Potato Ale

This Irish red ale is made with organic potatoes for an exceptionally rich, smooth body.

Preheat the oven to 300°F (150°C). Season the beef with salt then sear it in a pan with the oil, making sure to caramelize all sides of beef. Add onions, celery, carrots, and caramelize. Once golden brown, add garlic and tomato paste and cook for 2 minutes, stirring constantly. Add the rest of the ingredients and top up with water or stock so all meat is covered in liquid. Place a lid or tinfoil on the pot and braise in the oven for 4 hours, or until the beef is fork tender. Cool to room temperature, then transfer the meat onto a sheet pan and put it into the fridge. Strain the stock, return to stove, and simmer to reduce by half. Set aside.

Mushrooms: Place garlic heads in a small frying pan with water and duck fat. Place a lid or tinfoil over the pan and cook at 300°F (150°C) for 35–40 minutes or until tender. Remove to cool, then squeeze out cloves.

Add 1 Tbsp olive oil to two separate pans, warm up, then add equal amount of shallots to each pan. Keep on medium heat and cook until tender. Add 2 cloves of roasted garlic to each pan, then add all of the mushrooms to one pan, sautéing quickly until tender. When mushrooms are almost ready, add the spinach to the other pan; cook until just wilted—don't overcook. Take off heat and set aside.

In a small pot warm up the beef in the braising liquid.

Eggs: Heat another medium pot of water to simmering and add cider vinegar. Crack eggs into the simmering water and poach for about two minutes or until just set. Take eggs out and set to drain on a dry cloth or paper towel.

When beef is hot and ready to serve, add herbs and butter. Stir until the sauce is reduced to a nice glaze.

To finish, put a mound of spinach in the middle of a plate, place beef on top, and scatter mushrooms around the beef and on top. Finish it off with the poached egg and serve!

Short ribs

4 (6 oz) pieces boneless
   beef short ribs
1 Tbsp olive oil
¾ tsp salt
2 medium onions,
   roughly chopped
1 (4 inch) piece of celery,
   roughly chopped
2 medium carrots, roughly
   chopped, cut into thick slices
3 large garlic cloves,
   finely chopped
1 Tbsp (15 mL) tomato paste
4 fresh parsley stems
4 fresh thyme sprigs
2 bay leaves
4 cups water or beef stock
1 Tbsp (15 mL) butter
4 heads garlic, top cut off
½ cup (125 mL) water
1 Tbsp duck fat
4 garlic cloves, roasted
2 Tbsp (30 mL) olive oil
2 shallots, minced
3 big handfuls yellow foot
   mushrooms (or other
   wild mushrooms)
4 big handfuls spinach
2 Tbsp (30 mL) cider vinegar
4 eggs
1 Tbsp (15 mL) Italian
   parsley, chopped
1 Tbsp (15 mL) thyme, chopped
1 Tbsp (15 mL) Italian
   parsley leaves
1 Tbsp (15 mL) butter

JASON LEIZERT

he offers a collection of artisanal flavours of the highest quality—something this town had not yet seen. Salamis, hams, and bacon, this man goes whole hog—down to jars of high-quality lard for sale. Farm-raised, antibiotic-free pork is delivered to his shop for processing and he, in Old World style, utilizes the whole beast.

With a fabulous cheese selection (including local and imported), mouthwatering house-made pickles, salad dressings, meats, and sausages, the Brick is the place to hang.

And Jason is a man with a big heart. After spending time working at Save-On Meats on East Hastings in Vancouver, he is very aware of the homeless population and is sympathetic to its needs. He was part of a successful initiative at Save-On Meats that helps feed the homeless by selling customers tokens for hot breakfast sandwiches, which they can give to people in need. Here, he has founded the Bag Lunch Program. Each week he and his volunteers put together bagged lunches with a sandwich, a baked good, an apple, and a juice box and hand them out to the local homeless in the downtown area.

🐦 @saltedbrick   f /saltedbrick   saltedbrick.com

The Chef ✤ Jason Leizert
The Salted Brick, Kelowna

The Farmers ✤ Sara & Troy Harker
Harker's Organics, Cawston

The arrival of the Salted Brick on Kelowna's main drag, Bernard Avenue, marked a significant change to the city's urban culture. It is a cool, casual place with cozy, urban-chic décor and an open kitchen. It offers delectable choices for breakfast, lunch, snacks, and dinner . . . and then there is the house-made charcuterie.

No stranger to the restaurant scene, Jason Leizert was part of two highly successful restaurant projects in Vancouver (Boneta, The Parker) and also spent time at the retro-hip butcher shop Save-On Meats on East Hastings Street (you know, the one with the flashing neon pig sign). Leizert honed his butchery and charcuterie craft over the years in Europe and

"As fifth-generation farmers it is our passion and goal to carry on the legacy set forth by previous generations. It is our passion to feed people, to create a secure sustainable food system, and connect consumers to their farmers."—Sara Harker

The winners of the BC Outstanding Young Farmers 2013 award, Sara and Troy Harker are continuing their family's legacy and taking it to the next level in expanding their organic reach. Sara explains, "We are now the second-largest organic tree fruit packer and shipper in Western Canada. We have been working very hard to get more organic BC product on store shelves and have branched into CO-OP stores from Alberta to Manitoba.

LEFT TO RIGHT: AKAYA HARKER, MOMMY SARA HARKER, KAYDENCE HARKER

REBECCA KNEEN & BRIAN MACISAAC

This year, 2016, marks our 60th year of retail business, and it will also be the 100th birthday of the Fameuse/Snow Apple Tree!" The ancient Snow Apple (or Fameuse) tree, planted in the early 1900s, still stands on the Harker Organic Farm and is a proud symbol of the Harker family's pioneer heritage.

The family has an interesting history: The Harker (née Manery) family settled in the Similkameen Valley and began farming in 1888. Ancestor James Manery and his wife travelled west on horseback from Ontario in 1868. The first of their ten children, Samuel James Manery, was the fourth non-native baby born in the Similkameen.

Sara speaks on the future of Okanagan farming: "We see that there will be a reintroduction of food production, both tree fruit and ground crops in the coming years. As there was a surplus of grapes on the market, we hope that this results in farmers reverting back to tree fruits, planting varieties with high demand that will help fulfill the need for local Canadian fruit domestically. There has been a strong trend with an increase in demand for organic produce across the country. We hope that we organic farmers can persuade conventional farmers to convert due to the economics of organic farming."

Sara is a busy lady. She is mom to two adorable girls, and is also the winemaker at the farm's now-certified-organic Rustic Roots fruit winery. Plans for the future include an organic bistro on the farm.

f /HarkersOrganics   🐦 @HarkersOrganics   harkersorganics.com

The Beer Makers ✤ Brian MacIsaac & Rebecca Kneen
Crannóg Ales, Sorrento

So much more than a brewery, Crannóg Ales is a model of sustainability and creativity, and continues to demonstrate the power of positive activism. Brian MacIsaac and Rebecca Kneen founded the beautiful property, which had a building "with the bones of something already there," Brian says. Those bones would become the brewery. Crannóg Ales is Canada's first certified organic farmhouse microbrewery, one of only a few in the world. They grow their own hops and offer a program encouraging new growers that includes a how-to manual when they purchase plants. Brian is also proud of a new variety of hops they developed on the farm, named Sockeye Hops for the salmon running in the river nearby. Brian and Rebecca are all about community and cultivating the organic growing community. Currently, they have offered their property as an incubator to help others get started in farming.

Brian spent many years in Belfast, where his roots lie. There he honed his many gifts, including design. An artist, he paints, sculpts, and designs incredible tattoos! There is a gallery on the farm to visit after your beer cravings have been sated in the tasting room.

f /Crannóg-Ales   crannogales.com

Paleo Pumpkin Pancakes

SCOTT NYSTROM

BEV WIENS

RAINA DAWN LUTZ

The Paleo diet is based on the types of foods early humans (or cave people) are presumed to have eaten. For Scott Nystrom of Nourished Edible Wellness, using the best local ingredients is key to making any dish great, and local pumpkin makes these pancakes shine. He wants to prove that one does not have to go without when living the Paleo way!

Serves 2 (about 8–10 pancakes)

Enjoy with Raina's Kombucha

This fermented drink is super popular and a healthful choice. On its own, it tastes like mellowed vinegar with notes of tea, but it can be enhanced with other natural flavours.

Preheat oven to 350°F (180°C). Quarter and seed pumpkin. Bake skin side up for 35 minutes or until soft. Carefully scoop pumpkin flesh from skin and purée in blender. Measure out ½ cup (125 mL) and save the rest for a curried soup.

In a blender, mix pumpkin purée, eggs, vanilla extract, maple syrup, and coconut oil.

Add coconut flour, spices, and powders. Blend. Let batter rest for 5 minutes so the coconut flour can hydrate and thicken the mix. While batter is resting, preheat pan on medium heat to ensure even cooking. Add a teaspoon of coconut oil and swirl it around the pan. Give the batter a quick blend again to ensure an even consistency.

Pour batter into small puddles around the pan, and expect the batter to spread out a bit. Smaller 3-inch (8-cm) pancakes are best as they cook faster and are easier to flip. When bubbles begin to appear and edges of pancakes are golden, carefully flip and finish cooking. Due to the high egg-to-coconut flour ratio in many Paleo recipes, pancakes may still be a bit wet on top when you flip them, so be careful not to splash molten batter.

Serve stacked high with fruit and nuts, grass-fed butter or coconut butter, and drizzle thoroughly with maple syrup.

Chef's note: You might want to double the recipe, as leftover pancakes freeze well, and make for easy grab-and-go toaster snacks. Just pop a frozen pancake in the toaster and grab a banana to go. Uncooked batter also keeps well in a vacuum-sealed bag in the freezer for one month.

1 small pumpkin

4 medium free-range eggs

1 tsp (5 mL) vanilla extract

2 Tbsp (30 mL) maple syrup

2 Tbsp (30 mL) coconut oil, melted (plus more for frying)

2 Tbsp (30 mL) coconut flour

2 tsp (10 mL) cinnamon

½ tsp (2.5 mL) ginger

¼ tsp (1 mL) nutmeg

¼ tsp (1 mL) cloves

¼ tsp (1 mL) baking soda

¼ tsp (1 mL) baking powder

Suggested toppings: maple syrup (real deal only) berries, apple butter, coconut butter, grass-fed butter, nuts and seeds, banana slices

LEFT TO RIGHT: SCOTT NYSTROM & BEV WIENS

The Chef ❖ Scott Nystrom
Nourished Edible Wellness, Kelowna

Kelowna-based Scott Nystrom is a holistic chef whose company, Nourished Edible Wellness, focuses on culinary nutrition and holistic chef services. He is an advocate of farm-to-table cuisine and explains, "Holistic nutrition is all about the mind-body-spirit connection between ourselves and our food. As a holistic chef, I care about not only how my food tastes and looks, but where it came from, how it was raised, and how it makes you feel. The soil stewardship necessary to cultivate the sweetest pumpkin; the diet and well-being of the milking cow that gives the cream for

my organic grass-fed butter; the farmers worldwide who toil to produce my maple syrup, sea salt, and cinnamon—all the care and attention that goes into each ingredient before it even reaches my hands is infused with love that you can taste." Cooking is about family, and cooking with your children inspires them. He recalls, "Some of my earliest memories are of crawling underneath my grandma's butcher block table and listening to the sound of her knife chopping, the rhythmic tap on the wood as she wielded her blade like a culinary magician. She always smelled and tasted everything as she cooked, and coaxed me to smell it too. The love my grandma put into her food inspired me to become a chef."

Originally from the Kootenays, Scott came to the Okanagan to finish a degree in sociology at the University of British Columbia Okanagan (UBCO) with a focus on cultural theory and the sociology of food. He shares, "I was raised in and out of a camper-ized school bus in the Kootenays, moving more times than I am years old, and when my family came to the Okanagan in 2000, I could never have imagined that somewhere could feel so much like home. Now, my beautiful wife and two incredible kids inspire me to celebrate real food daily as we cook, dance, and laugh together in the kitchen. Kids are the farmers and chefs of tomorrow. Inspire them to know their food."

f /the-nourished-chef   thenourishedchef.ca

The Farmer ❖ Bev Wiens
Stepney Hills Farm, Armstrong

Bev and Robin Wiens are familiar faces at the Kelowna Farmer's Market. Their Stepney Hills Farm stand offers a beautiful range of local, certified-organic produce. Bev is a huge part of the market (in both Kelowna and Armstrong) and is currently the acting president of the Kelowna Farmers' Market board. She is a leader we can trust to keep a market that features the best farmers the Okanagan has to offer.

Both Bev and Robin had farm values instilled

in them as children. Bev says, "As a child I spent many summers at my paternal grandparents' farm in Saskatchewan. Nothing was wasted. Food scraps and grains grown on the farm were fed to the animals that, in turn, fed the family with meat, dairy, and eggs. Animal manures were composted and used to fertilize and improve the soil that vegetables were grown in. My husband was raised on a farm; we always dreamed about getting back to farming, but making a living and raising a family delayed the dream. We bought our farm in 1989, but continued to work off the farm while producing hay and raising a few cattle and pigs. Our home garden kept expanding until we decided to let go of our paycheques and followed our dream of full-time farming. It has been challenging and rewarding at the same time. Becoming certified organic was the only way to go for us. That is how my grandparents and Robin's parents farmed their land. Anyone can make claims that they don't spray or use chemicals, but customers can rely on 'certified organic' because the farms are inspected and the records are checked by an independent verification officer before the farmer receives their certification—and every year after that. That is an expense to us, but it's worth the cost to assure the public that products purchased from us are grown by Canadian organic standards."

f /stepney-hills-farm   soilmate.com/farms/stepney-hills-farm

RAINA DAWN LUTZ

The Kombucha Maker ❖ Raina Dawn Lutz
Lutz Nutrition, Penticton

Raina Dawn Lutz is a holistic nutritionist and self-appointed "fierce fermenter." She offers products, consulting services, and online services and programs, including weight management. Raina's story: "When I was studying holistic nutrition in 2010 in Kitsilano, Vancouver, one of my school peers taught us how to brew our own kombucha. She told us tales of her bubbling, popping, fizzing, brewing, fermenting kitchen at home. I envisioned her as a mad scientist in the kitchen. The more I learned about fermented foods, the more I became obsessed with having my own mad scientist kitchen. When I moved back to the Okanagan after studying, it was first on my list to get everything going: sauerkraut, pickles, apple cider, traditional ginger ale, and of course kombucha. I found the more I made, the more people asked for it, and Experience Kombucha was born. Teaching classes keeps my interest high; I love watching others learn to ferment their own foods. The transformation is magical, each and every time."

🐦 @rainadawnlutz   lutznutrition.ca

Kombucha*

Heat water on the stovetop. Once it reaches a slow boil, remove from heat. Add tea and sugar and stir. Steep for 5–10 minutes. Remove tea bags. When tea is room temperature, add to glass fermenting container. Add the mature kombucha starter and the kombucha mother. Cover with clean tea towel and leave to ferment in a safe, warm spot, ideally 70–85°F (21–29°C). Do not shake, stir, or otherwise disturb the brew during this time. After a few days (in the summer) up to a week (in the winter) begin tasting the brew. The longer it sits, the more acidic it will become. When the flavour is to your liking, bottle it and refrigerate. Raina pours the brew into old wine bottles or other bottles with tight lids. Store the 'mother' SCOBY with more fresh tea and sugar in a jar; do not refrigerate. Pass the 'baby' ('baby' will look like a thin film, and will form the shape of the container it's in). The mother will produce one each batch, so pass it on to a friend so they can start their own; you can also compost it, or simply leave it and continue brewing another batch.

After bottling, add a few tablespoons of herbs or fruit for flavouring, and set on counter (with a lid on tight) for 12–24 hours. Off gas (remove cap to release gas) at least once, ideally twice (especially if leaving for 24 hours), strain (optional), then refrigerate. Waiting a week or two before drinking often gives more carbonation. Enjoy chilled.

Health benefits: Fermented foods give us those "good bacteria" we are always hearing about. We need these healthy microbes for our immune systems, proper digestion, and mental health.

*This recipe requires a kombucha starter culture called a SCOBY (which stands for "symbiotic colony of bacteria and yeast").

1-gallon (4-quart) glass container (for fermenting)
2 Tbsp (30 mL) loose tea or 8 tea bags (black or green)
1 cup (250 mL) organic cane sugar
13–14 cups (3 L) water
2 cups (500 mL) starter tea or white vinegar

Sunshine Farm Heritage Potato Flan

MONA JOHANNSON

THE ALCOCK FAMILY

DAVID PATERSON

This delicious flan is a favourite for chef Mona's lucky guests at Sunshine Farm, an educational farm owned by the Alcock family. The Alcocks grow beautiful vegetables, mostly heirloom, heritage, and unusual varieties—this due to dad Jon Alcock's passion for seed saving and learning about heritage varieties. Each potato variety has a fascinating history, as do most of their products. This special farm is a delicious lesson in the importance of preservation and growing with love.

Serves 6

Enjoy with 2014 Rosé, Tantalus Vineyards

Red delicious apple, wild mixed berries, and an intriguing grapefruit edge make this wine both a summer patio quaffer and a complex and subtle dinner wine.

Preheat oven to 450°F (230°C).

Combine the eggs, mixing gently with a fork, leaving the mixture streaky. Season with salt and pepper.

Heat skillet and fry prosciutto on medium-high heat until lightly crispy (3–4 minutes), then set aside.

Using an ovenproof skillet, heat 2 Tbsp (30 mL) of the olive oil over medium-high heat. Layer the potatoes in a circular pattern, alternating colors, in the bottom of the skillet. Drizzle with the additional 1 Tbsp (15 mL) of olive oil and fry until the potatoes are crisp on the bottom.

Remove the skillet from heat and layer the potatoes with the onion, garlic, prosciutto, chèvre, peas, and tomato. Pour the egg mixture overtop, making sure everything is covered evenly. Season with salt and pepper.

Bake for 6 to 8 minutes or until set. Remove the skillet from the oven and gently loosen the sides and bottom as much as possible. Invert onto a large platter and sprinkle with the fresh herbs of your choice, and additional chèvre and peas.

Chef's Note: When my garden allows, I often add a small salad of baby greens or arugula tossed in a simple vinaigrette right on top. —Mona

6 or 7 farm-fresh eggs

salt and pepper

4–5 slices (75g) thinly sliced prosciutto, roughly chopped

3 Tbsp (45 mL) olive oil

6 small to medium multicolored heritage potatoes, thinly sliced

½ cup (125 mL) onion, thinly sliced

2 Tbsp (30 mL) garlic, finely chopped

¼ cup (60 mL) chèvre (soft goat cheese) plus extra for garnish

1 cup (250 mL) fresh (or frozen) peas, plus extra for garnish

½ cup (125 mL) tomato, chopped

fresh herbs such as parsley, basil, or thyme

RUSS ALCOCK AND MONA JOHANNSON

The Chef ❖ Mona Johannson
Sunshine Farm, Kelowna

Mona's catering business, Earth to Table, does just that—she sources the highest-quality ingredients grown from the good earth on her family's farm, Sunshine Farm. Her parents, Jon and Sher Alcock, have tended this beautiful land in southeast Kelowna since 1987, with Mona and her brother, Russ, spending much of their formative years there—as Sher says, "28 years of farming, learning, and planting."

The family has been working together on the farm for many years in various roles, and next year Mona and Russ will be stepping up their responsibilities. The farm exudes love and is dedicated to nature and community. The family operates a working school for mentally challenged people, who come and learn skills to be able to join the workforce. A crew of friendly farm dogs interacts with the smiling kids and lends to the warm vibes.

But Mona's true love is cooking and she will continue to integrate her talents and passion into the farm in other delicious ways. "I personally have a vision of continuing to move the farm in a culinary direction, facilitating more events, and adopting my father's beliefs in using these as an important opportunity to educate. I am extremely grateful for my brother, and the fact that together we are able to carry on the important work our parents worked so hard to start. We simply could not make it work if we both weren't happy to be immersed in our respective roles. It's always been a family business, and Russ and I feel fortunate that it will stay that way for at least another generation—and hopefully more."

f /sunshinefarmseeds   sunshinefarm.net   earthtotable.mona@gmail.com

The Farmers ❖ Jon, Sher, & Russ Alcock
Sunshine Farm, Kelowna

Sunshine Farm is all about sharing, growing, and tending to the good earth and human connection. Jon and Sher Alcock, son Russ, and daughter Mona make up this family farm production. Sunshine Farm includes a certified organic vegetable and herb garden, a forest of pine and fir with marsh meadows, mow-land, and a small heritage apple orchard. The majority of its food crop and seed production is of certified organic heritage or heirloom varieties, and it is a giant in the heritage seed-saving world. It offers an organic seed catalogue, which is available on the website.

Jon, whom we privately refer to as the "Gandalf" of the soil, has also written a foreword to this book. His immense knowledge of the good earth is simply astonishing.

Mona and Russ will soon join in the farm operations full-time, continuing the family legacy. Mom, Sher, explains: "Passing operations along to the next

LEFT TO RIGHT: SHER ALCOCK, MONA JOHANNSON, JON ALCOCK

DAVID PATERSON AND ELLA

generation gives us great satisfaction and a reassurance that Sunshine Farm will continue to serve and grow for our community."

Russ shares, "I decided farming was my future after I felt I had enough of a career flying helicopters, which had me working three-weeks shifts and eating camp food. I would come back to our beautiful organic farm on my time off and would always have a tough time leaving to go back on tour. I love the diversity of my job; no two days are the same, and I work closely with the planet, which never stops changing and teaching me new things—plus I eat very well. The respect I have for my parents and what they have done with the farm is such that I don't anticipate any drastic changes in the future, aside from a few veggie varieties."

f /sunshinefarmseeds   sunshinefarm.net

unique terroir. The vineyard is impeccably managed and set on a historic, and incredibly beautiful, site in southeast Kelowna. It is formally owned and tended by Kelowna's Dulik family. (The view from Tantalus Vineyards is featured on the cover of this book!)

David says, "We continue to farm as sustainably as possible—without the use of herbicides or pesticides. Our honeybee apiary is thriving and we're amazed at the species diversity that can be found on our estate— including all that dwells within our mature, 10-acre forest at the centre of the vineyard. A naturally biodiverse vineyard and our LEED-certified winery are just two of the many ways we're working toward excellence in environmental sustainability."

f /tantalusvineyards   ✔ @tantaluswine   tantalus.ca

The Winemaker ❖ David Paterson
Tantalus Vineyards, Kelowna

For many, Tantalus has become the benchmark for fine Okanagan Rieslings, but it hasn't stopped there. All of the wines are exceptional and receive high marks from consumer to judge. Winemaker David Paterson is creating distinctive wines from the land's

Pepper Soup with Garlic Dumplings, Ricotta & Pickled Jingle Bells

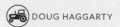 DOUG HAGGARTY

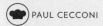 PAUL CECCONI

 DAVE & MELISSA DOBERNIGG

This soup is a perfectly peppery way to celebrate the huge variety of organic peppers grown at Fester's Organics, Doug Haggarty's farm in the mountains of Oliver. Chef Cecconi of BRODO Kitchen in Penticton utilizes two varieties of the whopping 40-plus varieties that Doug grows in this recipe, and also replicates one of Fester's famous smoked paprika spices—a product that is "gold" to local chefs (and cookbook writers . . . wink) in the know. Make a peck of pickled peppers to garnish—not Peter's recipe, but Paul's.

Serves about 10

Enjoy with BX Press Cider's The Prospector

High tannin levels and other complex flavours make for a cider with deep character, layered aromatics, and a pleasantly lingering finish.

Roast peppers in a 400°F (200°C) oven till skin blisters, then place in bowl and cover with plastic wrap. After 10 minutes uncover and peel the paprika peppers and then set aside.

Turn down oven to 350°F (180°C). Cut the heirloom tomatoes into wedges and toss with extra virgin olive oil and a light seasoning of salt and pepper. Place in a roasting pan in one layer. Roast for 30 minutes; remove from oven to cool.

In a large soup pot, sweat onions in 2 tablespoons (30 mL) of the butter on medium heat until softened; lightly season with salt and pepper. Add in the celery and garlic and cook, stirring, for 5 minutes. Add the smoked paprika peppers, chicken stock, and tomatoes. Simmer for 20 minutes. Add in fresh thyme and honey. Using a hand blender, blend in the other 2 tablespoons (15 mL) of butter until soup is smooth. Season to taste.

Fresh Ricotta: Line a sieve with cheesecloth and place over a large bowl. Slowly bring milk, cream, and salt to boil in a saucepan, stirring often. At boiling point, add lemon juice. Reduce temperature to low and simmer until the mixture curdles. Remove from heat and pour mixture over cheesecloth. Let drain 1 hour.

Roasted Garlic Dumplings: In a food processor, purée the garlic cloves and set aside. Add the butter, water, and salt to a saucepan and bring to a boil. While stirring, add the flour and cook until the mixture is smooth and detaches from the side of the pan. Remove from heat and cool for 10 minutes.

Continued on page 32

12 Fester's paprika peppers (red bell peppers can be substituted), roasted & smoked

2 cups (500 mL) heirloom tomatoes, roasted

2 Tbsp (30 mL) extra virgin olive oil

salt & pepper

2 medium onions, diced

2 Tbsp (30 mL) butter + 2 Tbsp (30 mL) for blending

1 celery rib, diced

2 Tbsp (30 mL) garlic, minced

8 cups (2 L) chicken stock

1 Tbsp (15 mL) fresh thyme, chopped

1 Tbsp (15 mL) honey

Fresh Ricotta (Makes about 2 cups [500 mL])

8 cups (2 L) 2% milk

1 cup (250 mL) whipping cream (36%)

½ tsp (2.5 mL) salt

3 Tbsp (45 mL) fresh lemon juice

Roasted Garlic Dumplings

1 cup (250 mL) garlic cloves, roasted

½ cup (125 mL) butter

1 cup (250 mL) water

1 tsp (5 mL) salt

1 cup (250 mL) flour

3 eggs

Continued from page 31

Mix in the roasted garlic purée evenly, then add the eggs, one at a time, while continuing to stir until blended.

Bring a pot of salted water to a simmering boil. Transfer dough to a piping bag and pipe small, 1-inch (2.5-cm) dumplings into the water, making sure not to add too many at a time—just enough to give each some space. When the dumplings float, remove with straining spoon, and transfer to a plate.

Pickled Jingle Bells Peppers: Cutest pepper name ever! Use this recipe as a side to your charcuterie platters or an accoutrement for sandwiches, fish tacos, egg dishes . . . whatever suits your fancy.

Place sliced peppers in a large heatproof bowl. In a large saucepan, bring all the remaining ingredients to the boil, then turn down and simmer for 10 minutes. Pour the hot pickling mixture over the peppers and let sit at least 24 hours to develop the delicious flavours.

To assemble: Place one heaping tablespoon of fresh ricotta and a few dumplings in each serving bowl. Pour soup over and top with pickled Jingle Bells. Devour with gusto.

Pickled Jingle Bell Peppers

6 lbs (2.75 kg) Jingle Bells peppers, cut into rings

2 cups (500 mL) water

4 cups (1L) apple cider vinegar

1 cup (250 mL) sugar

3 star anise pods

1 tsp (5 mL) fennel seed

1 Tbsp (15 mL) mustard seed

LEFT TO RIGHT: DOUG "FESTER" HAGGARTY & PAUL CECCONI

It's a family business. Paul's wife, Holly, is very much involved in the restaurant when she is not with their two young children. BRODO screams "welcome!" with its cozy décor, and this chef is never without a smile. It is obvious that he is doing what he loves, and that includes sourcing his ingredients locally.

"We have made several great relationships with local suppliers/farmers in the Okanagan and it is important to us that we support them," says Paul. "They provide us with some of the highest-quality products you can get, and it comes direct from the source, cutting out any middlemen."

On his relationship with Doug Haggarty of Fester's Organics, Paul explains, "I met Doug several years ago, and from the first time I spoke with him and sampled his product, I knew I wanted to support him and his business. He is passionate about what he does and works to accommodate any requests we ever have."

Brodo means broth in Italian and is a nod to Paul's family background. On his philosophy, Paul says, "As a chef it is my obligation to make myself loud and proud in promoting a farm-to-table philosophy and educating people to do the same."

f /tastebrodo   🐦 @tastebrodo   tastebrodo.com

The Chef ⁜ Paul Cecconi
BRODO Kitchen, Penticton

Since he was crowned Ocean Wise Seafood Chowder Champion in 2011, chef Paul Cecconi's name has been synonymous with soup. Recently he has become the host chef for the Okanagan's third chapter of the Soup Sisters/Broth Brothers charity (soupsisters.org), which makes soup for the local women's shelter.

Inspired by his mother and grandmother's Tuscan cooking, Paul trained to be a chef through Vancouver Community College's Culinary Arts Program. After travelling and working in restaurants in Australia, Vancouver, and Summerland, his dream of opening his own digs came true in May 2013 when he opened BRODO Kitchen in Penticton.

The Farmer ⁜ Doug Haggarty
Fester's Organics, Oliver

This wonderful character owns and operates a certified organic farm in the hills of Oliver, BC, and specializes in growing organic peppers and microgreens. He is a legend in his own right—chefs seek him out, some with great trouble, to get his products on their tables. Doug grows over 40 varieties of peppers in the ground and now also has a greenhouse operation that produces some of the most pristine microgreens I have ever seen. He delivers his products himself, to ensure they arrive fresh and perfect, and always leaves a trail of laughter behind him. He says, "Having your certified organics delivered to you personally by the grower to your place of business or function speaks to honest, upfront, personalized service and quality. It's just our way of saying thank you."

Describing how he came into organic farming from working on a ski hill and bartending, he says, "I was broke, I was starving, and no one wanted to hire me." This same checklist came up later in the conversation when I asked him another farm-related question.

Doug grew up in a tiny town called Decker Lake, near Burns Lake up north, where he spent his childhood fishing and hunting in the great outdoors and gained an appreciation for good food. He knows a lot about the quality of food, whether it's foraged, wild, or farmed. He says, "I love growing healthy food for people."

On a sustainable note, Doug also preserves and dries many of his products, and his incredible spice blends have gained a small cult following. He loves what he does—all of it. It is hard work, but he hires a couple of workers each season, many of whom return the next year because of the great fun they have working with and learning from him.

f /festersorganics   festersorganics.com

The Cider Makers ✤ Dave & Melissa Dobernigg
The BX Press Cidery & Orchard, Vernon

Both born and raised farm kids, Dave and Melissa Dobernigg now own and operate Dave's family farm in Vernon together with their three little girls. Dave is the third generation in his family to grow apples on this land, with generations before him that tending soil and crops in Europe. This is a farming family in the truest sense and they say, "Our dreams are tied inseparably to these trees, this land, this life on the farm."

Maintaining the orchard history of the Okanagan is important to this family, and choosing cider apples to grow was a brilliant choice. Quickly gaining a cult following for their unique products, the BX Press Cidery is a celebration of the orchard and our rich tree fruit history in the Okanagan.

Melissa beautifully describes what they believe in: "Our own hearts are in the orchard and we feel

DAVE & MELISSA DOBERNIGG WITH THEIR THREE DAUGHTERS

thankful to have such tangible work on such a beautiful piece of the earth. We believe in hard work, real food, and simple living—we trust these values are expressed in the quality of our apples today and are evident in the authenticity and calibre of our ciders."

The name of the farm and cidery also carries a great history: 6,000 acres of property in Vernon has the prefix BX, which stands for Barnard's Express & Stage Line—one of the oldest, largest, and longest running stagecoach companies in North America.

f /thebxpress   🐦 @thebxpress   thebxpress.com

Hot & Cold Curry Bowl with Coconut & Lemongrass Gelato

PATRICIA GUEST

THOMAS TUMBACH

HAGEN KRUGER

This curry is actually the first dish that chef Patricia created for the L'Oven menu. She explains, "I find the juxtaposition of flavours, colours, textures, and temperatures really interesting: spicy and hot; cool and creamy; yellow, green, and red; crunchiness, chewy noodles, and rich coconut and lemongrass-infused gelato melding with cilantro pesto drizzle. Introducing savoury gelato to new palates is fun too!"

Serves 4

Enjoy with 2014 Mystic River Gewürztraminer, Wild Goose Winery

Features intense floral, citrus, mineral and rose petal notes. Good acidity
helps to carry the flavours for a lingering, wonderful finish.

Add coconut milk, lemongrass, and lime leaves to a saucepan and heat to a simmer. Add lime juice, rind and honey and stir. Remove from heat; cool in a cold water bath.

Allow flavours to infuse for at least an hour and up to 4 hours. Strain and then add to an ice cream maker to process in the freezer, or process manually in a bowl, beating with a wooden spoon every 10 minutes until desired consistency is reached.

Chef's note: About half of our customers prefer a sweeter gelato. If you would prefer it to taste more like a dessert (and you can serve this version as dessert), add up to ½ cup (125 ml) of sweetener, stirred in when the infusion is hot.

Curry: Soak rice noodles in a bowl of cold water. Sauté vegetables in hot oil, tossing to coat. Add curry paste and coconut milk. Reduce to thicken. Salt to taste. Bring a pot of water to a boil. Drop the soaked noodles into a colander to drain and then transfer into the pot of boiling water for 1 minute to soften. Pour back into colander and shake to help drain water. Transfer noodles to a large bowl and add the vegetables and sauce. Toss to coat noodles. Dish into four bowls, top with two small scoops of gelato, and chopped cilantro to taste.

Gelato

4 cups (1 L) coconut milk

¼ cup (60 mL) lemongrass, chopped fine

4 lime leaves (available at Asian markets frozen if you cannot find fresh)

4 Tbsp (60 mL) fresh lime juice plus the rind

2 Tbsp (60 mL) honey

Curry

1-lb (500-g) package rice noodles

⅔ cup (150 mL) or 2 medium carrots, julienned

⅔ cup (150 mL) or 2 small stalks celery, julienned

12 small mushrooms, quartered

1 cup (250 mL) or 6 leaves sui choy

⅔ cup (150 mL) or 1 medium red and/or yellow pepper, julienned

2 tsp (10 mL) olive oil

4 Tbsp (60 mL) yellow curry paste

1 cup (250 mL) coconut milk

salt to taste

1 bunch cilantro, chopped, for garnish

PATRICIA GUEST

promote local organic produce and agritourism. I had every single school kid in the district, from kindergarten to grade three, on my farm every year from 1996 to 2003—2,800 kids. I dressed like a pumpkin and showed them how bees tell other bees where the good stuff is by doing the bee dance. My son is 17 and is the first generation to be raised on GMO-free foods for his entire life."

f /LovenFoodDrinksMore   (778) 754-7070

The Chef ❖ Patricia Guest
L'Oven Farm Fresh Food, West Kelowna

Patricia Guest is an authentic locavore. A chef, a farmer, a teacher, and an activist for the preservation of the good earth, she is an advocate and leader for the local food movement. She is a driving force in promoting a healthy farm environment and healthy food. And, she dances while she cooks.

Patricia explains, "Food is my life. It's been my lifelong passion, the base for much of my creativity, writing, photography, cooking, floral design, landscape design, and the foundation of most of my income."

She swore she would never open a restaurant; however, destiny arrived in the shape of a building for lease in 2015. L'Oven embodies Patricia's passions for local farm-to-table food. Everything here is made from scratch, with ingredients lovingly chosen and sourced from local farms and artisans. More than a chef and a food lover, Patricia is a food activist, passionately supporting anti-GMO campaigns—she wrote her first article against GMOs in 1997. Her ability to write and speak on the state of our local food and farming with such depth and wisdom comes from personal experience as a farmer. Patricia Guest was ahead of her time and a pioneer of sorts in our local movement. She adds, "I was the first market garden to be spray-free and to

The Farmer ❖ Thomas Tumbach
LocalMotive Organic Delivery, Summerland

This is a farmer with a bigger mission, or "motive," to be precise. Thomas Tumbach holds a degree in Agriculture and Sustainable Land & Food Systems from the University of British Columbia. His company, LocalMotive, which he started in 2005, is how he fulfills his goal "to help develop local food distribution networks that connect organic farmers with consumers in the interior regions of BC."

Thomas explains, "My dad was a farmer on the prairies, but really I was inspired to go into farming because I had always had an interest in biology and the environment. At university I did a degree in Agro-Ecology. The courses I took made me want to understand the social implications of agriculture as well, and the more I learned, the more I realized that food is the centre of our society. The more you learn about producing and preparing food, the more you realize that local is where the best food is at. Seasonal eating is an exciting and grounding experience, and it connects us to the environment we are surrounded by. Sure, I love to eat the occasional avocado, but really, I love to work with what is in season, and try to produce and procure the best selection and variety of locally available goods possible."

He, his wife Celina, and their four children own and operate the 10-acre Oasis Organic Farm in Summerland. "In the past ten years that I have run LocalMotive, I have seen an amazing shift in consumer

LEFT TO RIGHT: BROTHERS HAGEN & ROLAND KRUGER

THOMAS TUMBACH

awareness," says Thomas. "People are really starting to understand the broader implications of eating locally, and are realizing that they can have an impact on the core of our society if they eat more seasonal, local diets. I think this is a trend that will not go away; it will continue to increase in importance, and will definitely involve a new generation of smaller, locally supported farms. A younger generation of farmers and producers will need to step up, and they are doing that. I can't wait to see where we are at in another ten years!"

f /localmotive   localmotive.ca

The Winemaker ❖ Hagen Kruger
Wild Goose Vineyards & Winery, Okanagan Falls

The Kruger family's Wild Goose Vineyards is a pioneering Okanagan Falls winery that has won multiple awards for its fine wines, and set a benchmark for winemaking in the region. A humble and hard-working family, sons Hagen (winemaker) and Roland (general manager) now run the operations of the vineyard and winery, which were started by their father, Adolf Kruger, who purchased the property in 1933. Adolf named the vineyards for the large flock of Canada geese he saw on the property—as he approached, the flock of geese took flight and he felt this was an omen.

And indeed the vineyard and eventually winery would take flight. Adolf planted varietals from his homeland of Germany, focusing on Riesling and Gewürztraminer to start, and sold them to Mission Hill Winery. During the late 1980s, the movement began to allow smaller wineries to open offering "farmgate" sales. Adolf persisted in lobbying for this law to be passed and, as history tells, they were successful. In June 1990, Wild Goose Winery was the seventeenth winery established in British Columbia.

From then on, the winery continued to grow, the vineyards expanded, and the wines flourished under the meticulous hand of Hagen Kruger. Currently the winery holds over 300 medals honouring their wines and wine making. Wild Goose Vineyards has become a destination for wine lovers.

f /wildgoosevineyards   🐦 @wildgoosewines   wildgoosewinery.com

Medley Seasonal Tarte

JAY DRYSDALE

JEROME GAGNE

JAY DRYSDALE

BUDDHA

This is one of those dishes where you ask yourself, *Why didn't I think of doing this before?* It is versatile, beautiful, rustic looking, and screams "wine country living!" Puff pastry may be old school—but it never goes out of style because it's just so darn easy and delicious.

Serves 2, 4, 8, 10—depending on the course you are serving it as.

Enjoy with 2014 Westbank Gamay, Bella Wines

The salty, earthy flavours of this tarte balance perfectly with the crisp, tart rhubarb and grapefruit flavours of the Westbank Gamay sparkling wine.

Preheat over to 400°F (200°C). Mix together goat cheese and cream to a spreadable consistency. Roll out half of the puff pastry to ⅛–¼-inch (3–6 mm) thick, into the shape you like, and spread the goat cheese mixture over it. Slice your vegetables as thinly as possible (a mandoline works well), and arrange overtop the goat cheese. Less is more for this dish; if you put too many vegetables on top they will not cook through properly in the time it takes the puff pastry to cook. Place on a cookie sheet and bake for 10–15 minutes until the tarte is golden brown. Remove to cool.

While the pastry is cooking, make a lemon-Dijon vinaigrette. In a bowl, whisk together the Dijon mustard, lemon juice, and olive oil. You want the dressing to be tart to balance the richness of the pastry. Toss the vinaigrette with fresh arugula and then hand tear pieces of prosciutto into the salad. Don't forget to gently season with salt and pepper.

Chef's note: What I love about this recipe is that you can utilize whatever is in season. I like to use a goat cheese base for its tartness, but any spreadable cheese will work.

Once the tarte is out of the oven and cut the way you like, top with the arugula and prosciutto salad. Now you have the perfect wine country brunch/lunch, which takes less than 30 minutes from start to finish!

2–3 Tbsp (30–45 mL) goat cheese

1–2 Tbsp (15–30 mL) cream

1 4 × 4-inch (10 × 10-cm) piece puff pastry, rolled out

1 medium zucchini, cut into ribbons with vegetable peeler

½ small red onion, sliced very thin

½ medium potato, cut very thin

1 tsp (5 mL) Dijon mustard

1 Tbsp (15 mL) lemon juice

3 Tbsp (45 mL) olive oil

3–4 cups (1.5–2 lbs) loosely packed arugula

10 slices (150 g) prosciutto

salt & pepper

LEFT TO RIGHT: JAY DRYSDALE WITH BABY BELLA & JEROME GAGNE

important to my life and not just as sustenance. Your palate develops in this industry, and you truly appreciate the decadence that the sensory experiences of food and wine provide. Then my love of food turned me onto wine—how can you understand food if not for the beverage that's so closely related to it? This passion for food *and* wine allowed me to run wine stores to restaurants to wineries. Then harvest stole my heart and I knew this was the creative outlet I had always been looking for: farmer/chef/sommelier/winemaker—all of my passions captured in a bottle. It has allowed me to take a decade of food and wine experience and invest that into our own winery."

Jay continues: "Now our lifestyle is teaching us how to live off the homestead. From farm animals to growing fruits and vegetables, we are living as organically as we can. The dream is to be able to live off our land while producing world-class wines. Each year we gain more confidence in expressing vineyard definition in our wines while we embrace being students of the land. The next step is to build the ultimate outdoor kitchen that would entice any chef to coax out the beauty of local ingredients for intimate dinners. We would love to build the same appreciation of regional cuisine that is sought after in other wine regions found around the world."

f /BellaWines 🐦 @Bellawines bellawines.ca

The Chef ⚜ Jay Drysdale
Bella Wines, Naramata

Jay Drysdale and his wife/partner Wendy Rose are a wonderful example of a couple that has manifested its dreams. He's from the West Coast and she's from California; the two found each other among the chaos of wine country, fell in love, bought a vineyard, and built a winery together. This is no ordinary winery, either—it is the Okanagan's only boutique sparkling wine house and it found an instant cult following.

Jay is both a chef and winemaker; which passion came first? Jay explains, "My love of food came first, but it took me a while to realize that food was

The Farmer ⚜ Jerome Gagne
Medley Organics, Summerland

Jerome Gagne is a treat for chefs because of his passion for farming and growing and experimenting. "I love chefs. It's great to see and taste what they make with the produce I grow. They love what they do, and I love what I do, and the result comes out as beautiful meals," he says.

Thankfully, young farmers are finding a way to farmland that they could otherwise not afford to buy. He ended up finding a piece of land in Summerland to lease "where the smaller scale of my operations was a better fit to the smaller piece of land and accessibility to more restaurants and markets" he says. "The challenge facing farmers is always the marketing and sales. People interested in farming normally don't have issues when growing things. Selling them to make a living is where it gets more difficult. I have a good following of locals at the farmers' market and great chefs that appreciate my products and make my business possible. Tomatoes are my specialty, but I also grow lots of root vegetables (carrots, beets, onions, leeks, sunchokes, parsnips), some greens (kale, chard, lettuces, arugula, etc), and then beans, peas, cukes, squash, a few herbs, radishes, kohlrabi, peppers, and basil. And more. I tend to experiment a bit on new varieties of produce and then try new crops in small amounts for fun and for chefs. I grew peanuts this year. I learned that Ontario grows them, so I thought BC would be easier. I planted them a little too late so they didn't grow to full size, but fresh out of the ground they were very sweet, and roasted they were nice and crunchy. I might grow a few more next year and see if they grow a little fatter."

Email: jerome@medleyorganics.ca

WENDY ROSE AND JAY DRYSDALE

to pump out unadulterated bubbles. I need to stay true to a vintage and refuse to cave to industry norms to 'just add acid.' Buddha's blend is about making the best of this problem year. It is about expressing vintage variation and not something I want Bella fans to think might be a regular thing. This was the hottest year on record for at least 50 years, so hopefully we won't have a blend again for a very long time." *Ohmm . . .*

f /BellaWines 🐦 @Bellawines bellawines.ca

The Winemaker ✤ Jay Drysdale
Bella Wines, Naramata

Jay Drysdale's boutique sparkling wine house crafts and labels its wines by region, clearly allowing the distinct expression of each terroir to be experienced. Bella Wines is also a member of Garagiste North Festivals (a wine festival featuring winemakers creating small lots/under 2000 cases of wine) and the only sparkling one too! (For more on Garagiste North, see page 105.)

Stay tuned for a new sparking blend coming in 2016: Buddha's Blend! It is named for baby Buddha the bulldog, but there is more to this story. Says Jay, "Buddhism shows us how to understand ourselves and how to cope with our daily problems. Last year, 2015, was a very tough year for a natural winemaker trying

Bean Scene's Best-Ever Ginger Cookie

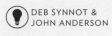

DEB SYNNOT & JOHN ANDERSON

AMY LANG

AL LANG

The team at Bean Scene Coffee Works has generously contributed its treasured ginger cookie recipe. Enjoy this melt-in-your mouth cookie with a Bean Scene cuppa—it's a perfect pairing. You'll experience, for at least a moment, the feeling that all is right in the world.

Makes 20 cookies

Enjoy with Bean Scene Espresso Graf bean blend

This chocolatey bean, with its notes of dark cherry, makes the

perfect espresso, cappuccino, latte or brewed coffee at home.

Preheat your oven to 375°F (190°C). Whisk the flour, baking soda, and spices in a medium bowl. Set aside. In a stand mixer, using a paddle attachment, beat butter, brown sugar, and ⅓ cup (75 mL) of white sugar together on high speed, until light and fluffy. Add the egg yolk and vanilla and continue mixing on a lower speed until blended. Add molasses and mix again for about 30 seconds. Scrape down the sides of the bowl and add the dry mixture, mixing on low speed until all the flour is incorporated. The dough will be soft and slightly sticky.

Roll dough into 1 tablespoon-sized balls and drop onto a plate containing ½ cup (125 mL) of white sugar. Roll cookies in sugar and press lightly to form a disk, making sure to coat both sides. Place on a parchment-lined baking sheet, spaced 1 inch apart. Bake 1 cookie sheet at a time on the middle rack for 11 minutes. The cookies should come out of the oven with their trademark crackle appearance and looking slightly under-baked.

Allow cookies to cool on the pan for 2 minutes before transferring to a wire rack to cool completely—or eat them hot from the oven alongside a cup of Bean Scene coffee!

2¼ cups (560 mL)
 all-purpose flour
1 tsp (5 mL) baking soda
1½ tsp (7.5 mL) cinnamon
1½ tsp 7.5 mL) ground ginger
½ tsp (2.5 mL) nutmeg
¼ tsp (1 mL) allspice
¼ tsp (1 mL) black pepper
½ tsp (5 mL) cloves
¾ cup (1½ sticks)
 melted butter
⅓ cup (75 mL) brown
 sugar, packed
⅓ cup (75 mL) white sugar +
 ½ cup (125 ml) for
 rolling cookies
1 large egg yolk
1 tsp (5 mL) vanilla
½ cup (125 mL) fancy
 molasses

JOHN ANDERSON & DEB SYNNOT

Deb Synnot and John Anderson moved here from the West Coast, changed careers, and bought the Bean Scene Coffee Works Downtown, where their love affair with brewing the coffee bean began. Now with two young daughters, Amelia and Esme, they have grown into a family of coffee houses with baker Amy Lang and coffee roaster Al Lang on board, Charlotte Augustine at the helm of Bean Scene Downtown, and Oliver Hall operating Bean Scene Big White. With more growth to come, this crew is definitely Kelowna's power coffee collective, and we love them.

Before Al took over, Deb explains, "John was lucky enough to be taught by Patrick Graf (our espresso is called Espresso Graf in honour of him). Patrick was the first micro-roaster in Vancouver; he sold his company to what is now JJ Bean. His conditions were simple: roast old school in small batches. Over time, we have changed our roasting style to put a greater emphasis on the inherent flavour a green bean brings to the table. Much like grapes, all the conditions in which green beans are grown and then processed affect the taste. Therefore, all of our medium roasts are single origin (one bean from one place). We use a couple of green bean suppliers that specialize in sustainability through buying from single-estate farms."

With their gang expanding, Deb has taken on the role of jumping bean, hopping from shop to shop, bakery to roastery—wherever she is needed—giving her more flexibility with her kids. John has passed his roasting hat to Al and is in the office handling the internal business works. All in all, this wonderful coffee culture is based on a laid back, happy workplace vibe that continues to keep its community alive and hopping.

f /BeanSceneKelowna   beanscene.ca

The Baker & The Coffee Roaster ❖ Amy & Al Lang
Bean Scene Coffee Works, Kelowna

Amy and Al have always been involved in the food industry in one way or another. Amy had been working as baker in the kitchen at Bean Scene headquarters for a couple years when she and Al were presented with the opportunity to run the shop at Capri Mall. They jumped on it. Amy and Al explain that Deb and John, who provided incredible support and hands-on training, are now like family. Bean Scene is a unique culture and a strong brand that focuses on building a strong team. Amy is now heading up the main kitchen, where the offerings are made with locally sourced, in-season ingredients (whenever possible), and "only real and pronounceable ingredients," like butter. No hydrogenated fats are used. The menu includes the usual cafe sweet treats, but also has light lunch options, like panini sandwiches, and delicious healthy alternatives, like the Buddha Bowl—great options to take back to the office for lunch. And they even use sustainable packaging.

Takeaway is good, but this group wants you to sit and stay awhile. Amy says, "It's all about the ritual of coming into the shop, standing in line chatting, and then sitting down and watching the world go by. Taking ten minutes from your day to recharge."

The great news is another shop is soon to open in the cool Pandosy neighbourhood!

f /BeanSceneKelowna   beanscene.ca

AL & AMY LANG

Bill's Spirited Apricot Brandy Jam

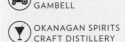

BILL WALKER

PENNY & ANDREW
GAMBELL

OKANAGAN SPIRITS
CRAFT DISTILLERY

Bill Walker is the jam master at Okanagan Grocery Artisan Breads, Kelowna's favourite bakery, which owns with his wife, Monika (known as Monika the Baker). This delicious local jam, with its addition of brandy, will take your toast to another level. Or serve atop pancakes or French toast with crème fraîche for a Sunday brunch that is *très elegant*.

Makes six to seven 1-cup (250 mL) jars

Enjoy with Okanagan Spirits Apricot Brandy (and coffee)

Add a ½ shot or more to your cup of coffee, topped with some whipped cream, for a delightful coffee cocktail at brunch or at the end of a long day.

Sterilize jars and lids as per manufacturer's directions. Keep jars and lids hot until ready to fill.

Remove pits from washed apricots and chop finely. Place fruit and lemon juice in a large, nonreactive pot. Bring slowly to a full boil. Add the pectin and return to boil. Incorporate sugar and return to boil. Stir occasionally to ensure no fruit sticks to the bottom of the pot; do not over-stir. When the mixture begins to resemble jam texture, and sheets off of a spoon, add brandy. Boil for an additional minute.

Pour jam into hot, sterilized jars. Clean rims of jars, apply lids, and screw on bands. Place jars in canner for 10 minutes. Store in a cool, dry place.

Bill's preference is to use a kitchen scale for jam making, primarily using a ratio of 1:1 for sugar to fruit (for this recipe, substitute 1 kg sugar and 1 kg apricots for the amounts listed above). If substituting pectin varieties in this recipe, please be sure to follow package guidelines. Happy jamming!

6–7 one-cup (250-mL) jars and lids

3½ lb (1.6 kg) apricots, chopped

2 Tbsp (30 mL) lemon juice

2 Tbsp (30 mL) powdered pectin

5 cups (1.2 L) sugar

⅓ cup (75 mL) Okanagan Spirits Apricot Brandy

LEFT TO RIGHT: ANDREW GAMBELL, MONIKA & BILL WALKER, PENNY GAMBELL

The Jam Maker ❖ Bill Walker
Okanagan Grocery Artisan Breads Bakery, Kelowna

Okanagan Grocery Artisan Breads Bakery in Kelowna is owned and operated by Bill and his superstar baker wife Monika. "Bread ingredients are selected for their organic, local, and flavour properties; you'll find no mixes, loaf pans, or preservatives here. From grainy ryes and naturally leavened sourdough loaves to one-of-a-kind bread recipes," (like killer brownies, buttery croissants and bagels, to name a few), they also carry other locally inspired and created gifts in their shops,

supporting their many friends in the industry. They also carry an array of seasonal jams that fly off the counter, and Bill is the man behind those sweet jars of preserves.

This is a second career for Bill; his previous was with a successful Internet company. Bill explains, "Jam-making is such a rich experience—the steps involved in transforming the raw fruit into the hot jam allow time for both exploration and contemplation, and always result in a fragrant environment." And how about those soul-satisfying, popping sounds that the jars make when they are sealing? Must sound like symphony at the bakeshop on jam day.

What is wonderful for customers is their chance to enjoy homemade style jams made with local fruit—like that of long-time orchard farmer Penny Gambell and her family from Lake Country. Says Bill, "We met Penny at the Kelowna Farmer's Market a few years ago, and have had a great relationship ever since. The quality and consistency of her products are amazing. We look forward to getting various stone fruits from her farm each year."

When I first met Monika, I asked her how she could manage those night shifts baking. She said she loved the feeling that when everyone else was asleep, she was baking to feed her village. Bill continues, "It's hard not to love your business, when it is an environment where people freely share their creativity and talents and are also enthusiastic about helping one another. On another level, being one contributor to such a large, wonderful community of customers, restaurants, and other partners is particularly satisfying as well."

f /okanagangrocery   🐦 @okanagangrocery   okanagangrocery.com

The Farmers ❖ Penny & Andrew Gambell
Gambell Farms, Lake Country

A fourth-generation family farm in beautiful Lake Country, BC, Gambell Farms began in 1963 when Pearce Gambell purchased the land. He and his wife, Penny, worked hard to grow the business and purchased another farm in the 1970s. That land, on what is now Okanagan Centre Road, is now a thriving roadside market. Pearce has since passed on, and son Andrew has taken the lead but still works closely with his mom, Penny, to run the successful farm and farm-stand operations. The Gambells, known for their tremendous tree fruit production, also offer vegetables at their roadside market and at the Kelowna Farmer's Market. The variety produced on the prolific 30-acre farm is fantastic—from a wide array of tree fruits and vegetables to delicious, hard-to-find Saskatoon berries to homemade treats, like Penny's sought-after fruit pies.

Have a question about agriculture, produce, or politics? Ask Penny. She is deeply entrenched in Okanagan agricultural industry, having held significant political positions in the past and present; she has been a councillor-at-large with the Lake Country City Council since 2015. Her impressive history includes serving as a commissioner with the Agricultural Land Commission from 1991 to 1995, and, from 1992 to 2004, working with the BC Fruit Growers' Association, where she was president from 2000 to 2004. Penny is also a past president of the Canadian Horticultural Council (CHC), the national organization that represents a broad base of horticultural needs and issues. Before that she was a secondary school teacher and raised three children!

250-766-4036

PETER VON HAHN

Well, life gave Frank apples, apricots, pears, cherries, and more so he made spirits.

The original distillery remains in Vernon. The new owners, the Dyck family, opened a second location downtown Kelowna. The range of spirits is fantastic and their repertoire even includes the fabled Absinthe made by wormwood.

Master distiller Peter von Hahn has also created delicious liqueurs from unique local products, like sea buckthorn berries, haskap berries, and now huckleberry. Whisky and a single malt scotch whiskey have also joined the repertoire with great acclaim.

Tours and tastings are available at both locations. Kelowna also houses the Barrel Room Lounge and Patio, where a list of classic cocktails, flights, and drams of award-winning whiskeys can be enjoyed.

f /okanaganspirits   ✗ @okanaganspirits   okanaganspirits.com

The Spirit Maker ❖ **Peter von Hahn**
Okanagan Spirits Craft Distillery, Kelowna

The Okanagan Spirits Craft Distillery story is a lesson in innovation and sustainability. The original owner and master distiller, Frank Dieter, was inspired to utilize the leftover tree fruits that were discarded after harvest for being damaged or those that were left to rot on the ground due to weather damage or neglect. It's an example of another Old World principle in action, sort of like "if life gives you lemons, make lemonade."

What is an Artisan?

The abundant sunshine, the clear lakes and rivers, and the rolling agricultural lands practically hit you in the face in the Okanagan. Therefore, it's easy to think that these are the main ingredients in the bounty of food that surrounds us here. Landscape, soil, and climate, however, are merely the start. It takes a community of people who care deeply about good, healthful, tasty food. It's the steady hands and the strong backs of the artisan farmers, fishers, foragers, cooks, chefs, brewers, distillers, and winemakers that turn those natural assets into great Rieslings, silky Pinot Noirs, perfectly ripened heirloom tomatoes, and oh-my-god peaches, cherries, apples, and pears.

What is an artisan? Good question—the term is used rather indiscriminately these days. At its root, it's about the art and craft of growing, raising, or producing great food and wine. Artisans take their time. They risk failure for a vision. They accept effort, struggle, and perseverance. Artisans grow and create in small batches. They're hands-on and obsessed with quality. They know there are no shortcuts to the best flavour possible. And this is what makes their products so unique and delicious.

Lucky for us, the Okanagan has long attracted artisan farmers, cheese makers, bakers, chefs, foragers, brewmasters, distillers, and winemakers who are dedicated to creating the best food and drink possible. Their skill and passion are the heart and soul of the world-class culinary scene that we now have in the Okanagan region.

But this is all just talk. You'll know it when you taste it. You'll hear it in the stories. You'll feel it in the experience. Best of all, you'll find edible definitions of artisan products from top to bottom in the Okanagan and Similkameen valleys.

JENNIFER COCKRALL-KING
Author, Food Artisans of the Okanagan: Your Guide to the
Best Locally Crafted Fare (TouchWood Editions, 2016)

Original
Garlic Scape
Salt

Wood Fired — Oven Roasted

farmendsotter organics
Cawston, BC

CERTIFIED ORGANIC
Eggplant

STARTERS

Okonomiyaki

 JUNYA NAKAMURA

 TERUO & MUTSUKO OGI

JAMES & JOANNA SCHLOSSER

I experienced a *wow* moment when I first tasted the okonomiyaki on chef Junya Nakamura's menu at Wasabi Izakaya. Like most of his creations, it was a totally new flavour experience. This once-humble pancake-style dish is sort of a catch-all in the home kitchen, and a very homey, common dish in Japan. It is now an Izakaya favourite, one that you will see trending on menus. Feel free to incorporate other vegetables, shrimp, chicken—whatever you have on hand.

Serves 4

Enjoy with 2014 Small-Batch White, Niche Wine Co.

This wine is summer in a bottle. The bold acidity of the Riesling, the rich roundness of the Pinot Blanc and the freshness of the unoaked Chardonnay join forces in the fight against monotony.

Mix the special sauce ingredients together in a bowl and set aside for serving.

Mix all of the pancake ingredients together in a large bowl and let sit for about 5 minutes to combine. Heat oil in a large frying pan until it starts to smoke. Add "pancakes" to the hot pan—roughly 1 cup (250 mL) per portion, or, if you are adventurous, you can make one big one; it will just be harder to flip. Take a peek underneath and when they are golden brown, flip the pancakes, and reduce heat to low. Cook for another 6 minutes. Do not push the pancake down or touch it. After 6 minutes remove from the pan and drizzle with Junya's special sauce.

Pancakes

6 cups (1 lb) cabbage, shredded

2 tsp (10 mL) baking powder

1 cup (250 mL) flour

¾ cup (175 mL) water

1 large egg

¼ cup (60 mL) pickled ginger
   (pink sushi ginger) (optional)

2 Tbsp (30 mL) soya sauce

2 Tbsp (30 mL) canola oil

Special sauce

½ cup (125 mL)
   Worcestershire sauce

½ cup (125 mL) ketchup

¼ cup (60 mL) mayonnaise

1 tsp (15 mL) brown sugar

LEFT TO RIGHT: TEREO & MUTSUKO OGI & JUNYA NAKAMURA

are everywhere; Junya describes them as "a casual drinking establishment that serves tapas-style food and drinks—basically a Japanese pub." This is no sushi restaurant; the dishes are creative and exciting, and although there are still a few sushi rolls on the menu, they are far from the usual.

Junya sources all of his vegetables locally, and looks to the Ogi family in Rutland as his main source. Widely known and loved, Mr. and Mrs. Ogi are famous for their roadside market and farm. Junya explains, "All the vegetables there are picked on the day they are sold. There is something about their vegetables that tastes different from other local vegetables. Is it the soil? The experience? I can feel the love of Ogi when I use their products." Junya described their vegetables' uniqueness as coming from the terroir—vegetables, just like grapes, take on flavours from the land and weather conditions. But I think the love also counts big time.

f /wasabi-izakaya   𝕏 @wasabiizakaya   wasabi-izakaya.com

The Farmers ❖ Tereo & Mutsuko Ogi
Ogi's Greenhouse, Kelowna

For over 40 years, Mr. and Mrs. Ogi have offered locals fresh, naturally grown produce and bedding plants, and they have a huge, loyal customer base. Starting with buying their bedding plants in the spring, customers continue to visit Ogi's Greenhouse throughout the season to buy the wonderful vegetables.

The Ogis purchased the land in 1973. They raised three children on that farm, all grown now with university degrees, and they are so proud. They also move like they are in their twenties, and do the bulk of the work on the farm themselves. It is miraculous—and they are the picture of health! Mr. Ogi believes that working in the soil gives him energy. Hard work, fresh air, and exercise—that is the farmer's workout.

The Ogis' land is tended naturally, including hand weeding, which yields them prolific crops and healthy plants. Visitors to Ogi's Greenhouse know they are

The Chef ❖ Junya Nakamura
Wasabi Izakaya, Kelowna

Junya Nakamura opened Wasabi Izakaya in 2008. Born in Osaka and raised in Osaka and Hyogo, Japan, Junya moved to Maple Ridge in 1992 with his family when he was 13. After finishing high school, Junya took a job at Guu Izakaya, one of Vancouver's hottest Japanese restaurants, as a dishwasher. His plan was to do this temporarily to save money for university. Something clicked and the restaurant business became his new passion.

The Izakaya craze has been building for a long time on the West Coast, but in the Okanagan, Wasabi Izakaya is the only one of its kind. In Japan, they getting the very best quality product available. Mrs. Ogi has been known to grab a vegetable that is not quite to her standards out of a customer's hands and replace it with a better one. She also knows the perfect variety to use in whatever dish you tell her you are making. Mr. and Mrs. Ogi are two of the sweetest people you will ever meet. They are so generous and welcoming, you will want to become a regular here.

250-765-8050

JOANNA & JAMES SCHLOSSER WITH BABY HUGH

The Winemakers ❖ James & Joanna Schlosser
Niche Wine Co., West Kelowna

James and Joanna Schlosser's wines pack a wallop! Using grapes from James' parents' vineyard high up in the hills of West Kelowna, the Hugh and Mary Vineyard, the couple has injected their hard work and passion into this wine-making project and it has paid off—the wines are excellent and receiving fantastic reviews and a small collection of awards already.

Producing less than two thousand cases, they currently qualify as "Garagistes," for the Garagiste North Wine Festivals (for more on Garagiste North, see page 105), although the future holds an expansion, "but we don't think we will go over 3,000 cases," says James. He wants to keep it real and be hands-on in both the vineyard and the cellar.

The couple and their adorable little guy, Hugh, are having a wonderful time building their new business on the vineyard. They recently made a full move to the Okanagan from Vancouver after both managing careers through commuting. Their new space has an amazing new event area formed high up above the vineyard that offers remarkable views of the valley and Okanagan Lake. They are also experimenting with a delightful new work crew: baby doll sheep that will help manage the pruning. They are also looking into some chicken employees to help scratch and fertilize the land. All in all, the Schlosser's have definitely found their Niche in life.

f /niche-wine-company   🐦 @nichewineco   nichewinecompany.com

Family-Style Wise Earth Tomato Salad

CHRIS STEWART

JOHN HOFER &
BRENDA PATERSON

DARRYL BROOKER

This dish by Chris Stewart of the Mission Hill Family Estate Winery in West Kelowna is a dazzling celebration of the beloved tomato. The colours of Wise Earth Farm produce are otherworldly, making this dish a visual work of art. It's delicious and easy to make, too. The leftover pear dressing is wonderful on salads or veggies.

Serves 4

Enjoy with 2013 Terroir Collection, No. 16 Southern Cross
Sauvignon Blanc, Mission Hill Family Estate Winery

The epitome of crisp minerality benefiting from partial French oak fermentation. Mid-weight with layers of lime, guava, pink grapefruit, green apple and candied apricot. Gooseberry and tarragon mid-palate with a structured finish.

Make dressing: Combine pear and apple juice in a blender and purée until smooth. Add thyme and then seal in a Ziploc bag and massage to infuse aroma of the thyme into the pear, and let sit overnight. Strain thyme out of pear purée. Add vinegar and 5 Tbsp (75 mL) apple juice and emulsify by whisking in canola oil. Adjust seasoning.

Toss tomatoes in dressing and marinate for 2 hours before assembly.

Make roasted garlic purée: preheat oven to 350°F (180°C). Slice the bottom off 1 bulb of garlic and drizzle with 1 Tbsp (15 mL) olive oil. Place the garlic sliced-side up in a small piece of aluminum foil, cover with foil, and roast until the garlic cloves are tender (approximately 40 minutes). Remove the bulb from the oven and cool. Squeeze the cloves out onto a cutting board then use a large knife to scrape the cloves into a purée.

Mix together fresh ricotta, 1 Tbsp (15 mL) garlic purée, and verjus; adjust salt to taste.

To assemble: Spread ricotta and basil into the base of a platter. Arrange the tomatoes over the spread and serve!

1 large Okanagan pear,
   very ripe
½ cup (125 mL) apple juice +
   5 Tbsp (75 mL)
2 Tbsp (30 mL) thyme
5 Tbsp (75 mL) apple
   cider vinegar
1 cup (250 mL) canola oil
2 lb (1 kg) Wise Earth assorted
   small tomatoes, cut in half
1 garlic bulb
1 Tbsp (15 mL) olive oil
1 cup (250 mL) fresh ricotta
1 tsp (5 mL) verjus
   or lemon juice
½ cup (125 mL) fresh
   basil, chopped

LEFT TO RIGHT: CHRIS STEWART, BRENDA PATERSON & JOHN HOFER

Chris is passionate about supporting our local farming community and explains, "Sustainability, waste management, and carbon footprint are all topics that we pay careful attention to here at the winery. We invest a great deal of time sourcing ingredients that are produced, caught, or harvested in a sustainable and environmentally conscious manner."

Working at a winery provides chefs a unique chance to truly learn the art of wine pairing. Chris says, "I have started looking at dish construction differently since starting at the winery. I have been fortunate to receive wine training from some amazingly talented people and it has driven my consideration to balance, weight, and textures in the dishes to allow for a pairing that both complements and enhances the wine."

f /Mission-Hill-Terrace-Restaurant   🐦 @MH_Terrace   missionhillwinery.com

The Chef ✤ Chris Stewart
Mission Hill Terrace Restaurant at
Mission Hill Family Estate Winery, West Kelowna

Now the executive chef at Mission Hill Family Estate Winery, Chris Stewart has had an incredible culinary journey since he graduated from Prince Edward Island's Holland College, one of the best cooking schools in Canada. His resume includes time spent at Thomas Keller's über-famous French Laundry restaurant in the Napa Valley, as well as at the legendary three-Michelin-starred restaurant, The Fat Duck, in the UK (named Best Restaurant in the World for two consecutive years).

Besides creating glorious dishes and sourcing from almost exclusively local products, Chris loves to teach and has expanded the culinary cooking class program at Mission Hill. In his role as executive winery chef, he also provides mentorship for his team at the Terrace Restaurant and designs the curriculum for Mission Hill's culinary education program.

The Farmers ✤ John Hofer & Brenda Paterson
Wise Earth Farm, Kelowna

John and Brenda at Wise Earth Farm are the epitome of modern, ethical farmers. Unable to afford land of their own, they have leased a piece of property and built a flourishing garden/greenhouse operation.

John grew up on a farm in Alberta, but never planned to pursue agriculture as a career; Brenda was raised in Vancouver with no connection to gardening or farming at all. Brenda recalls, "At some point John read a book by John Jeavons called *How to Grow More Vegetables: Than You Ever Thought Possible on Less Land than You Can Imagine* (a book about bio-intensive square-foot gardening), and was inspired by the idea of being able to farm without having to have a large amount of land." Thus their dream of farming was born.

Brenda explains, "Finding land to farm was easy for us. Through a friend of John we were introduced to Ryan Markowich, and we offered to farm his field, which is a two-acre portion of his property. We started farming a small portion of Ryan's land five years ago and have increased every year to where we now utilize the entire two-acre field.

Our approach to farming is to maximize our growing capacity while utilizing the best organic growing methods available. We have found that when a plant is healthy and is not under stress, it resists disease naturally. We use the square-foot gardening method on a large scale. We have 290 garden beds that are 50 feet long by 2.5 feet wide (125 square feet) with 1-foot-wide pathways in between. An onion requires 16 square inches of growing space, so we plant over 1,000 onions in a 125-square-foot bed. Romaine lettuce requires 64 square inches of growing space, so we plant approximately 250 romaine heads in a 125-square-foot bed."

Stewart and John and Brenda have built a working relationship based on mutual respect. "It's been a pleasure to work with chefs in the community that are as passionate about food as we are. We work closely with chefs to communicate what is available and coming in and out of season. Because we are an urban farm, we have the benefit of our chefs being able to visit the farm on a regular basis," says Brenda.

Wise Earth participates in the Kelowna Farmer's Market and it also offers a community supported agriculture (CSA) program, delivering seasonal harvest boxes to its members.

f /wiseearthfarm   wiseearthfarm.com

The Winemaker ❖ Darryl Brooker
Mission Hill Family Estate Winery, West Kelowna

Mission Hill Family Estate Winery is the Okanagan's most grand winery experience. Originally established in 1966, its renowned owner Anthony von Mandl purchased it in 1981 and transformed the estate into a stunning and dramatic European-style chateau featuring a landmark 85-foot-high bell tower.

Darryl Brooker assumed the role of chief winemaker in 2015. Prior to that he spent five years at CedarCreek Estate Winery, now a sister winery in Van Mandl's wine empire. Mission Hill now has estate vineyards in each of the Okanagan Valley's five growing regions to draw from, and Brooker works closely

DARRYL BROOKER

with James Hopper, director of viticulture. The Legacy Collection includes Oculus, Mission Hill's signature, multi-award winning Bordeaux-style wine.

Darryl says, "There's no better place to be making wine than here at Mission Hill Family Estate in the heart of the Okanagan Valley. Our range of vineyards up and down the valley—some of which are now over twenty years old—as well as our talented viticulture team and state-of-the-art winery have positioned us to bolster the international reputation of Mission Hill and the Okanagan Valley as one of the world's premier wine estates."

f /missionhillwine   ✔ @MissionHillWine   missionhillwinery.com

Cold or Hot Cucumber Soup with Gabe's Summerhill Honeycomb

 EZRA CIPES

 GABE CIPES

 ERIC VON KROSIGK

This beautiful soup is a celebration of organic farming, right down to the honeycomb garnish. The creator of this recipe, Luca Paola, who spent a year at Summerhill Sunset Bistro in Kelowna as executive chef, loved working with Gabe Cipes's garden produce, herbs, and honey, and was never at a loss for inspiration or ingredients on Summerhill's magical, organic, biodynamic vineyard/farm. Alex Lavroff, Summerhill's new chef, will undoubtedly exult in this bounty as well. You can taste the love and purity of nature in this soup, and can serve it warm or cold to best suit the season and your mood.

Serves 4

Enjoy with 2011 Cipes Blanc de Franc, Summerhill Pyramid Winery

Aged en tirage for 3 years, this well-balanced, sparkling wine provides notes
of eccles cakes, currants, dried raspberries and blueberries, finishing dry.

Blend first 3 ingredients in a high-speed blender to a smooth purée. Season with salt and pepper to taste. Use immediately or store in airtight container for up to 3 days.

Carrot salad: Slice carrots in half. Thinly slice on extreme bias. Add sliced carrots, scallions, and cucumber to a mixing bowl. Add lemon olive oil, lemon juice, and salt. Mix well and use immediately.

Pine nut mayonaise: In a high-speed blender, add all the ingredients and process until a mayonnaise consistency forms. Salt to taste. Thin as needed with water. Mixture will thicken as it sits. Store in the refrigerator for up to one week.

To assemble: Place honeycomb in centre of bowl. Place ¼ of the salad on top to add some height. Ladle a quarter of the soup around the salad. Drizzle about 1 tsp (5 mL) of the olive oil and 1 Tbsp (15 mL) of the pine nut mayonnaise in a ring around the salad. Sprinkle microgreens all over the soup. Finish with fresh cracked black pepper.

2 English cucumbers,
   peeled and cut into 1-inch
   (2.5-cm) spears
1 Tbsp (15 mL) lemon juice
1 Tbsp (15 mL) lemon olive oil
sea salt and pepper to taste

Carrot salad
1 medium purple carrot, peeled
1 medium white or yellow
   carrot, peeled
1 medium orange carrot,
   peeled
1 Tbsp (15 mL) scallions,
   thinly sliced
5 thin slices of cucumber,
   quartered
1 Tbsp (15 mL) lemon olive oil
1 tsp (5 mL) lemon juice,
   freshly squeezed
pinch salt

Pine nut mayonnaise
½ cup (125 mL) raw pine nuts,
   soaked in water for
   6–12 hours in fridge
2 Tbsp (30 mL) extra
   virgin olive oil
1 Tbsp (15 mL) lemon juice,
   freshly squeezed
pinch salt
2 Tbsp (30 mL) filtered water

Garnish
4 1-inch (2.5-cm) cubes of
   honeycomb
1 Tbsp (15 mL) olive oil
1 Tbsp (15 mL) fresh
   micro tarragon or
   red amaranth leaves
pepper, freshly cracked

LEFT TO RIGHT: GABE CIPES, EZRA CIPES & LUCA PAOLA

The Winery Maker ❖ Ezra Cipes
Summerhill Pyramid Winery, Kelowna

It's not easy to define Ezra Cipes. He is a rare, compelling blend of Old World ideals and New Age beliefs, and has the unmistakable gift of leadership borne from a passionate vision, integrity of purpose—all carried through the charm and ease of a true gentleman. He has become a strong and clear voice for the Okanagan wine industry, and is trusted for his fair and ethical philosophies and progressive ideas. Ezra officially joined the senior management team at Summerhill in 2008. During his tenure, he has received impressive accolades and awards, both locally and internationally. Becoming BC's first vineyard to achieve biodynamic Demeter certification in 2012 was an enormous achievement, which set the stage for Ezra to follow his and his father's dream of a biodynamic, organic future and deliver on their promise of 100% organic wine. Although Ezra grew up surrounded by wine culture, his first love was music. A singer, songwriter and musician, his legacy continues through his and his wife Rio's young daughter Ruth (aka 'Rockin' Ruthie').

f /summerhillwine   🐦 @summerhillwine   summerhill.bc.ca

The Bee Farmer ✤ Gabe Cipes
Summerhill Pyramid Winery, Kelowna

Gabe Cipes, a natural farmer and a bee farmer, is also a permaculture designer and the biodynamicist at Summerhill Pyramid Winery. He cares deeply about the earth and listens to and watches Mother Nature, allowing her to guide him. Setting up a bee colony on Summerhill's organic land has been a joy for Gabe, and is an integral cog in the natural ecosystem that is thriving under his hand. Gabe's knowledge of the land is impressive. He explains his passion: "I was drawn to work with the land by the intrinsic knowledge that everything is interconnected. My work is endlessly fascinating. I have had the opportunity to work with traditional ecological knowledge keepers of the Syilx territory here where we live. The indigenous teachings are of the relationships between the plant, animal, and subliminal worlds; biodynamics stem from the same knowing. *Bio* means life, and dynamics are the relationships.

"Last spring I split my three healthy colonies into eighteen new colonies and brought them to other organic farms hoping to build up honey production for next season. I brought most of them back to Summerhill by early summer and watched the populations grow throughout the season. The gardens we've been planting, along with the wild spaces we preserve at Summerhill, are having a positive impact on the bee populations. We also have a breeding yard on site that has supplied many nucleus colonies for new beekeepers all over the valley.

"Life begets life. I believe that the biodynamic farm organism with diversified crops of food and medicine with animal integration can feed and heal the planet and be resilient. We can design our environment to catch and store water and energy. Everything is interconnected and we need to integrate rather then segregate. I believe we can individually rediscover an evolved paradigm of life that lives in harmony with the natural rhythms of the earth and cosmos. Our individuality is at the centre of the farm organism."

f /summerhillwine 🐦 @summerhillwine summerhill.bc.ca

ERIC VON KROSIGK

The Winemaker ✤ Eric von Krosigk
Summerhill Pyramid Winery, Kelowna

The Cipes family, who founded and operate Summerhill Pyramid Winery, are certified organic champions. Father Stephen Cipes purchased their Kelowna vineyard back in 1986, with a crystal clear vision to transform the property to be certified organic. He speaks of a dream to have an "organic Okanagan."

Master winemaker Eric von Krosigk oversees the organic winemaking. The Summerhill vineyards are being raised biodynamically, allowing the most natural occurrence of vine management, which allows the ultimate terroir to be expressed through the grapes.

Famous for the pyramid built on the estate, Summerhill Pyramid Winery has become a leader in the certified organic/biodynamic grape growing movement. Euro-trained Summerhill wine master Eric von Krosigk is a minimalist winemaker, and explains, "We're down to six things that we use to make wine with, and that includes the grapes and yeast."

f /summerhillwine 🐦 @summerhillwine summerhill.bc.ca

Parmesan & Panko-Crusted Eggplant with Fresh Tomato Basil Sauce

GIULIO PICCOLI

DAVID NELSON & LISA MCINTOSH

SAL D'ANGELO

Chef Giulio Piccoli of One Big Table in Kelowna grew up in Italy and beautifully imparts the flavours of his homeland into the dishes he creates in his new home. The eggplant is a well-loved ingredient in Italy, but here people tend to not know what to do with it. This is an easy and delicious way to serve your local eggplant Italian style!

Serves 4

Enjoy with 2011 Tempranillo Miscela, D'Angelo Estate Winery

Begins with spicy blackberry and vanilla aromas. On the palate there is blackberry, boysenberry, dark chocolate and vanilla, with a lingering finish of spice and vanilla.

Season each side of eggplant rounds with sea salt. Place on a towel to drain while preparing the other ingredients. (This step is important to draw out the bitterness that eggplant can hold).

Meanwhile, whizz the tomatoes, basil, olive oil, and garlic in a blender until smooth; set aside. Crack the eggs and whisk in one bowl; mix together the panko and cheese in another. Fold the towel over the eggplant slices and gently squeeze to remove excess salt. Dip each slice in the egg mixture, and then in the panko/cheese mixture. Set on a cutting board or plate. Heat a non-stick frying pan to medium-high. Drizzle olive oil in the frying pan. When hot, add the slices to the pan. Cook on each side for 3–4 minutes or until golden brown. Remove from heat and set aside while you cook the remaining slices.

To serve, place the fresh tomato sauce in a small bowl in the middle of a serving plate, with the eggplant rounds spiraling around it. Top with freshly grated Parmigiano-Reggiano cheese and a few basil leaves.

Chef's note: That's it! It's simple and delicious—crunchy on the outside and creamy on the inside. And it will start your meal just right. Be creative with it—you can make the sauce with avocado and basil, or serve the eggplant in a sandwich. The possibilities are endless!

1 medium eggplant, sliced into ⅓-inch (8-mm) rounds

1 lb (454 g) tomatoes, quartered

10 basil leaves

4 Tbsp (60 mL) olive oil

1 clove garlic

2 eggs

1 cup (250 mL) panko (Japanese-style breadcrumbs)

¼ cup (60 mL) Parmesan (Parmigiano-Reggiano) cheese, grated

sea salt & pepper

LEFT TO RIGHT: DAVID NELSON, GIULIO PICCOLI, LISA MCINTOSH

we share the table with our farmers, our bakers, our butchers, and winemakers."

Giulio lives by the slow food philosophy, and thankfully, more and more, the Okanagan is beginning to adopt that lifestyle too. Says Giulio, "Growing up in Italy has significantly shaped my relationship with food. What I remember the most from growing up is the ritual behind the action of eating—setting up the table, the slower tempo, involving all the senses. It was an experience and not just an action, and this is what I always try to bring to our table today, even more than the food itself. My mom, of course, is still an endless source of inspiration in my life and in my kitchen. What I love about her the most is the simplicity she brings to the table. I always wonder how she manages to create such beautiful dishes with so few ingredients, and what I have learned is that she lets the ingredients speak to her. She listens; she pays attention to what's in front of her. And that's when magic happens."

f /onebigtable 🐦 @chefgiulio onebigtable.ca

The Shopkeepers ❖ David Nelson & Lisa McIntosh
Urban Harvest Organic Delivery, Kelowna

This wonderful couple is truly ahead of their time. Pioneers in the organic food home-delivery business, Lisa McIntosh and David Nelson set up their service way back in 2000, and have been supporting our local farm industry ever since. Lisa explains, "Urban Harvest was inspired by similar services in other towns and a keen desire to be part of a more sustainable, locally focused food system, plus the desire for meaningful self-employment. We wanted to create work for ourselves while helping to connect local organic farmers with local eaters, reducing the distance from field to table. It was also important to us to keep our service accessible and affordable to all—not only the elite—while maintaining fair prices for our suppliers."

Urban Harvest will deliver a weekly Harvest Box to your door filled with seasonal organic produce sourced

The Chef ❖ Giulio Piccoli
One Big Table, Kelowna

Giulio Piccolo left his beloved Italy to see the world at the tender age of 19. He ended up in Canada and found his way to the Okanagan where he took a job at a local restaurant. He stayed and has since gone on to create his own business: One Big Table. He caters and offers secret location pop-up dinners featuring seasonal, local cuisine, usually with a spin on the flavours of his homeland. Giulio explains, "We truly became our name: One Big Table that pops up in beautiful and sometimes unlikely places, like farms, bakeries, or even my own backyard. The focus, however, is still the same: we aim to close the gap between the producers and the consumers. We do that in a very simple way:

as locally as possible—and you can customize it to meet your personal tastes. And if you want to do the shopping yourself, you can hit their weekly warehouse store shop day on Saturdays. They are all about community and have built a wonderful network in the Okanagan. We know that consumers are paying more attention to where their food comes from and are shopping local more than ever. The other good news, says Lisa, is, "We have also seen a real shift in our local food system on the supply side as well! There are many more young folks starting out in farming (including urban farming) and other food-based micro-businesses, so the options for people to find local and organic produce have increased substantially since we started out 16 years ago."

"All that said, we believe that it's even more powerful to celebrate and support all that's good and healthy and nourishing in our food system, which is why we often sound like the cheer squad for our local organic producers! When people come to love and seek out good, real food from healthy sources, and are motivated to put a face to their food and learn where their food comes from, they naturally drift away from less life-sustaining foods. We try to act as a bridge by making good choices easily accessible."

f /Urban-Harvest-Organic-Delivery ✖ @urbanharvestok urbanharvest.ca

SAL D'ANGELO

thorough and passionate wine tasting lesson with all of his guests. The property has a wine shop and also a guesthouse with five units to rent on the vineyard.

This is a family business: daughter Stephanie manages the wine shop and guesthouse in Naramata, and son Chris operates the Ontario winery.

f /dangelowinery ✖ @dangelowinery dangelowinery.com

The Winemaker ✣ Sal D'Angelo
D'Angelo Estate Winery, Penticton

In 1983, Sal D'Angelo purchased his first vineyard in Amherstburg, Ontario. By 1999, his career in viticulture was affirmed when he won the title of Grape King, the top honour presented to the finest vineyard each year in Ontario. Sal decided to expand into the West and purchased a beautiful property on the Naramata Bench, where he has made his home. His connection to his wines and his vines is intensive and his wine making philosophy has always been "quality is grown." Sal is actually the first individual grower/vintner to produce wines in both Ontario and British Columbia. He is a delight to visit, and will share a most

Cheese Fritters with Okanagan Gazpacho

 VINCENT DENIS

 LEN MARRIOTT

 BRADLEY COOPER

Oh boy, these are good! Dipping the hot fritters into the chilled, spicy gazpacho makes for a taste bud party. This dish by Vincent Denis of Santé Bar & Grille and Roxy's Diner Food Truck can be served all year round—it works deliciously both on the ski hill or a hot Okanagan day.

Makes 10–12 fritters

Enjoy with 2014 Red Sky Rosé, Black Cloud Winery

This rosé is crisp and refreshing with aromas of spice, melon and strawberry. The finish lingers with hints of apricot and fruit leather.

Whisk together the eggs and yogurt. In a separate bowl combine the flour, baking powder, salt, green onions, and garlic. Combine the wet and dry ingredients until well blended. Slowly mix the cheeses in by hand. Form into small patties or log shapes as you wish. Roll in panko. Deep fry at 325°F (160°C) until golden brown (or pan fry in oil, flipping half way to achieve golden brown on both sides). Drain on a paper towel.

Gazpacho: Preheat oven to 450°F (230°C). Remove cores from tomatoes and place in a shallow pan. Sprinkle with 2 Tbsp (30 mL) olive oil and place in oven for 15–20 minutes until the skins loosen and turn brown. Remove from oven and cool. When cool, remove peels and combine tomatoes with all the other ingredients in a blender. Blend until smooth. Chill thoroughly, preferably overnight. Garnish with basil chiffonade and serve with warm cheese fritters.

Cheese fritters

2 large eggs
¼ cup (60 mL) Greek yogurt
1 cup (250 mL) flour
½ tsp (2.5 mL) baking powder
1 tsp (5 mL) kosher salt
¼ cup (60 mL) green onions, finely chopped
2 cloves fresh garlic, finely minced
1 cup (250 mL) French Gruyère, grated
1 cup (250 mL) Terroir Jurassic, grated
1 cup (250 mL) Terroir Continental Blue, grated
panko (Japanese-style breadcrumbs)
canola oil, for deep frying

Roasted tomato gazpacho

2 lbs (1 kg) fresh ripe tomatoes
2 Tbsp (30 mL) extra virgin olive oil
½ cup (125 mL) red bell pepper, chopped
½ cup (125 mL) cucumber, peeled, seeded, and chopped
½ cup (125 mL) red onion, chopped
1 medium fresh jalapeno pepper, seeded and diced
2 cloves garlic, minced
2 Tbsp (30 mL) apple cider vinegar
2 Tbsp (30 mL) Worcestershire sauce
½ tsp (2 mL) ground cumin
1 tsp (5 mL) kosher salt
½ tsp (2 mL) fresh ground pepper
2 Tbsp (30 mL) basil chiffonade, for garnish

LEFT TO RIGHT: VINCENT DENIS & LEN MARRIOTT

The Chef ✣ Vincent Denis
Santé Bar & Grille, Big White Ski Resort, Roxy's Diner Food Truck, Oliver

Vincent Denis and his partner, Christine Leman, wear two delightful restaurant hats. In the summer they are the duo behind the takeout window at Roxy's Diner Food Truck, and in winter, they (mostly he) operate Big White Ski Resort favourite Santé Bar & Grille, which they have owned for 13 years. Roxy's Diner has built a cult following with mouthwatering items, like chicken n' waffles and addictive poutine (FYI, Santé on the ski hill is famous for it too). Just two years old, the food truck is an exciting new addition for the restaurant team, which was used to taking summers off.

"We purchased Roxy's and redid the menu two years ago. A food truck seemed to be a great way to test the waters of the South Okanagan food culture without going full bore into a bricks and mortar restaurant," says Vincent. "The goal was also to be in a space where every bit of food that leaves the kitchen is prepared by me. I have had a passion for cooking since my mother showed me how to make a grilled cheese sandwich when I could barely see over the edge of the stovetop."

Vince is up at Big White working nonstop all winter, without even taking time to hit the slopes as the restaurant business is super busy. Christine doesn't enjoy the season on the hill and stays home in Oliver to operate her other side business, dog sitting. Vince says, "I would like to downsize to a smaller restaurant at some point in the future. I love Santé, but it is a very large operation. What operating the food truck has shown me is how much personal satisfaction I get from actually cooking and creating. I always have my eyes peeled for my next endeavour."

f /sante.grille   🐦 @sante_grille   santebarandgrille.com
f /RoxyFoodTruck   🐦 @taste_the_magic   roxysdiner.ca

The Cheese Maker ✣ Len Marriott
Terroir Cheese, Enderby

Len Marriott worked on dairy farms growing up, but ended up going to school to get his law degree. After a short time practicing, his passion for the farm drew him back. Len is now a cheese maker first, and a lawyer second. Len says the choice was easy: "I love the steadiness of it and I feel good about producing a high-quality product for the masses." He was inspired by the dairy farming industry at a young age when he was involved in the 4-H club's dairy program and went on to work at other dairy farms. Len says, "My favourite part of dairy farming is getting up at 4 AM and walking out to pasture to bring the cows in to milk." Len sees the huge potential for growth in the Northern Okanagan's agricultural sector. For as many wineries as there are in the South Okanagan, there are farms and farming initiatives happening in the north. His goal is to operate one small cheese plant on his farm with three or four other small dairy farms (with less than 100 cows each) providing the milk. Smaller production, smaller herds—it keeps the quality up and the animals are better taken care of.

Len uses the raw milk that comes from his cows—this is what makes his cheese special. He explains the name: "*Terroir* means from the earth. My cheese-making facility and cow rearing are 'beyond organic.'" He is following the European milk- and cheese-making method, including using 100 percent GMO-free feed, only local foraged hay, and adding no cornstarch to his products. He also only uses natural rennet. He says with his cheese products, "you are literally tasting the exquisite flavours of the North Okanagan and Shuswap!"

On his farm he has French Montbéliarde cows and makes six styles of cheese. Len plans to start an Okanagan cheese-making association and is going to begin experimenting with making fresh mozzarella to sell. Hooray!

f /terroircheese 🐦 @terroircheesec terroircheese.ca

The Winemaker ♣ Bradley Cooper
Black Cloud Winery, Penticton

Brad and his wife, Audralee Daum, are the proprietors of Black Cloud Winery, a high-quality, small-lot Pinot Noir specialist. Black Cloud is Brad's passion project and has received rave reviews for its six versions of the divine heartbreak grape, including a rosé. Black Cloud is a founding member of the Garagiste North wine festivals (for more on Garagiste North, see page 105), representing the Garagiste brand of small winemakers (under 2,000 cases) making big wines in the Okanagan—some in the garage, some virtual (without a tasting room), and some boutique. These winemakers all have the following in common: passion and damn good wine.

AUDRALEE DAUM & BRADLEY COOPER

Brad has received much acclaim in his past positions as full-time winemaker for some bigger brand wineries, and is now settled in at Serendipity Winery on the Naramata Bench.

f /blackcloudpinot 🐦 @blackcloudwine blackcloud.ca

Whipped Goat Cheese &
Walnut Streusel Phyllo Cups

GREG FUCHS

DONAT KOLLER

YVONNE KASUGI

MICHAEL CLARK

Featuring Happy Days Goat Cheese and Farmer's Dotter Garlic Scape Salt, these lovely individual tarts are loaded with flavour and make for a great starter to any meal.

Serves 12

Enjoy with 2014 Middle Bench Pinot Blanc, Clos du Soleil Winery

This Pinot Blanc is immediately appealing on the nose with zesty tangerines; lemons bind with light floral notes and a delicate frame of wet river stones. The palate is more of the same zing but with a rounder flavor of oranges and honeysuckle.

Preheat oven to 350°F (180°C). Make phyllo cups by brushing butter onto 1 layer of phyllo pastry at a time, stacking all 4 layers together. Cut the prepared phyllo into squares twice the size of the hole in a standard muffin tin. Turn a muffin tin upside down to mould the phyllo cups. While phyllo is still warm and pliable, form a square over every second tin mould, ensuring the phyllo is tight to the cup to prevent the cup from unravelling during baking. Bake in the oven until golden brown (approximately 10 minutes; watch closely as they tend to brown quickly). Carefully pull the phyllo cups free from the mould and let cool.

With a paring knife, carefully cut 1-inch (2.5-cm) notches into the beets and squash, forming petal-shaped pieces. Arrange them on separate pieces of parchment paper. Drizzle with a little olive oil, a good pinch of Garlic Scape Salt, thyme, and orange zest. Bake in the oven until squash is soft and beets are cooked through (30–40 minutes). Drizzle with some of the fresh orange juice. Set aside to cool.

Make streusel topping by mixing melted butter with flour and walnut until the ingredients are evenly combined and will hold its shape in small pieces. Bake in oven on a cookie sheet for about 15 minutes at 350°F (180°C) until golden brown. Set aside to cool.

In a Kitchen Aid mixer, whip together the goat cheese, whipping cream, a pinch of chopped thyme leaves, parsley, and a good pinch of the garlic scape salt for 2–3 minutes or until smooth.

Lightly season kale with a good pinch of garlic scape salt and enough olive oil to lightly coat. Fill each phyllo cup halfway with shaved kale. Pipe or spoon enough whipped goat cheese mixture to fill cups almost to the top. Arrange beets and squash flowers around the edge of the phyllo cups.

Spoon about ½ tsp (2 mL) of the chutney into the centre of the cup. Sprinkle some of the walnut crumble over the top and garnish with flat-leaf parsley.

Serve at room temperature.

1 package phyllo pastry
(thawed)
2 Tbsp (30 mL) butter, melted
1 medium squash (red curry,
hubbard, or butternut),
seeded, peeled, and
cut into "petals"
4 medium beets, peeled
1 orange, zested and juiced
2 Tbsp (30 mL) butter, melted
½ cup (125 mL) flour
¼ cup (60 mL) walnut pieces
1 cup (250 mL) Happy Days
soft goat cheese
¼ cup (60 mL)
whipping cream
2 fresh sprigs thyme,
leaves removed
1 bunch flat-leaf parsley,
chopped
2 bunches (4 cups, loosely
packed) kale, veins
removed, finely sliced
olive oil, as required
Farmer's Dotter Garlic
Scape Salt, to season
Gregor's Gourmet Golden Pear
Chutney (or similar)

LEFT TO RIGHT: YVONNE KASUGI & GREG FUCHS

The Chef ✤ Greg Fuchs
Gregor's Gourmet, Keremeos

Though he's originally from North Battleford, Saskatchewan, Greg says, "I ended up here by fluke. I took a break from culinary school in Edmonton, and came down to the Similkameen to pick fruit." He moved to the coast for a couple of years, but the beautiful valley drew him back. "I wanted to be closer to the food," he explains. He had been conjuring the idea of a food truck business for a while, so when he moved to Keremeos he already had a plan: "In 2009, the food truck scene was still in its infancy," he says, and his food truck catering business was an instant hit—not only for his innovative, cool mode of transportation and service, but also for his creative, locally inspired dishes.

"I enjoy sourcing the food and the connection with all the growers and producers. I am a farmer at heart and am happiest barefoot in the garden! I also enjoy preparing food with family and friends and the bond that it creates."

On describing his new home, he waxes poetic: "The Similkameen is sun-soaked orchards and fruit with a pinch of sage and a side of mountains."

f /gregorsgourmet   gregorsgourmet.com

The Artisan Salt Maker/Farmer/Baker ✤ Yvonne Kasugi
Farmer's Dotter, Cawston

The name Farmer's Dotter is a nod both to Yvonne's mom and heritage. Her mother is an organic grain farmer in Stockholm, Saskatchewan, and her ancestors come from Sweden, where daughter is spelled "dotter." Born and raised in North Battleford, Saskatchewan—like chef Greg Fuchs—Yvonne earned a degree in archeology, a passion she held since childhood. Marriage and jobs took her up north, near Charlie Lake, BC.

But then life changed. She got remarried to Morris Holmes, and after a call for help "one dark and stormy night" from her brother, who was running a fruit stand in Similkameen, they packed up and moved south. While Yvonne was working on her brother's farm, a neighbour with a woodfire oven and no bread-making skills asked for help. She obliged, and when she saw the neighbour's farm and gorgeous woodfire oven, she thought, *One day you will be mine!* And so in 2012, Yvonne and Morris bought that farm with the woodfire oven and garlic-planted fields, and their new career paths began.

"I've always baked bread," Yvonne says. "I grew up on homemade bread and made it for my own kids." The chance to bake multiple loaves in a woodfire oven sparked a new passion, and the business exploded. The garlic scape salt idea evolved from the property's prolific garlic crop; it produces seven tons of fresh garlic and leaves five tons of garlic scapes behind. A sustainable, recycling project turned out to have a delicious result. They roast the scapes in the residual heat of their woodfire oven, and source the salt, which is kosher, from an ancient hard rocks salt mine in Saskatchewan. "This salt is super pure because it is so ancient—it dates back to pre-human times!" she says. She aims to "keep the product 100 percent Canadian with a low-carbon footprint."

f /farmersdotter   🐦 @farmersdotter   farmersdotter.ca

DONAT KOLLER

MICHAEL CLARK

The Cheese Maker ✤ Donat Koller
Happy Days Dairies, Salmon Arm

Donat Koller, after graduating from agricultural college in Switzerland, found his passion in cheese and enrolled in cheese making college in 1993. He did not find the opportunity he was looking for in Europe and decided to immigrate to Canada with his wife, landing at a lovely farm in Salmon Arm. There, Donat decided that his future lay in goat dairy, and began his mission.

His operation has expanded over the years, and at one point he decided to focus on making the goat dairy products instead of raising the goats too—he leaves that to the farmers. Donat says, "The goat farmers are very involved in the structure of this company. Producing locally is important to us and gives consumers the chance to visit the farms and the processing facilities." This also guarantees their promise to make 100 percent, pure, natural, Canadian goat dairy products.

Happy Days Dairies maintains three dairy processing plants, with the original plant still on his farm in Salmon Arm, and has 12 dairy farmers under contract in British Columbia and Alberta. Donat says, "All three processing plants are located near our family farms, ensuring all fresh goat milk is processed immediately."

The name Happy Days Dairies was inspired by Donat's wife, Jasmine, who would sing the gospel song 'Oh, Happy Day' with her family at church. After meeting Jasmine, Donat was known to sing it once and a while too!

f /happydaysgoatdairy   ✔ @happydaysdairy   happydaysdairy.com

The Winemaker ✤ Michael Clark
Clos du Soleil Winery, Keremeos

Biodynamic, organic vineyard practice: this style of winemaking is alive and well in France, and is happily making its way to the Okanagan/Similkameen wine regions. Clos du Soleil is a biodynamic trailblazer in the Similkameen, and making award-winning, age-worthy wines to boot.

The name Clos du Soleil, a French term meaning "enclosed vineyard of the sun," refers to the rocks, soil, and sun, which together define this special vineyard. Founding owner Spencer Massie purchased the 10-acre vineyard on the Similkameen Valley's Upper Bench in 2005, planting the Bordeaux varietals of Cabernet Sauvignon, Merlot, Cabernet Franc, Malbec, Petit Verdot, and Sauvignon Blanc. Michael Clark is managing director and winemaker at Clos, taking over from Ann Sperling, who still consults for the team.

f /closdusoleil   ✔ @ closdusoleil   closdusoleil.ca

Wild Salmon Rillettes with Radish & Shaved Fennel Salad

 DANA EWART

 JORDAN MARR

 TYLER HARLTON

Dana serves these delightful rillettes with purple potato chips and radishes harvested from her friend Jordan's farm, but says that little crostinis would be just as nice.

Serves 6 as a starter

Enjoy with 2014 Viognier, TH Wines

The bouquet of stone fruit and crème brûlée lingers as this wine comes to life with minerality on the palate; the texture hints at the skin of a just-ripe apricot and carries through the finish.

Melt the butter and gently sweat the shallots until they are soft. Add the white wine and raw salmon and gently cook until the salmon has turned a lighter pink (about 2 minutes) then drizzle with Spanish brandy. The wine will reduce a bit and absorb into the fish.

Set aside to cool, then flake the cooked salmon and the smoked salmon together.

In a bowl, cream the butter and add the crème fraîche and lemon juice and zest. Stir until smooth.

Add the salmon and shallot mixture to the crème fraîche mixture, taking care not to break up the fish too much more. Chop the chives and fold them in. Add salt and white pepper to taste. Serve at room temperature with salad.

Salad: Finely dice the shallot, and juice the lemon. Combine shallot and lemon juice in a small bowl. Add a pinch of salt, and stir in the olive oil with a wooden spoon. Check for seasoning. Place the shaved fennel, slivered radishes, and fennel fronds in a bowl. Just before serving, add the vinaigrette to taste to the fennel and radishes. Toss well and season with a bit more salt to taste.

2 Tbsp (30 mL) unsalted butter

2 small shallots, finely diced

1 cup (250 mL) white wine

½ lb (250 g) wild salmon, raw

1 Tbsp (15 mL) Spanish brandy

¼ lb (125 g) wild smoked salmon

5 Tbsp (75 mL) unsalted butter, softened to room temperature

⅓ cup (75 mL) crème fraîche

2 Tbsp (30 mL) lemon juice + zest from 1 lemon

2 Tbsp (30 mL) chives

salt to taste

white pepper to taste

Salad

1 small shallot, finely diced

2 Tbsp (30 mL) lemon juice, freshly squeezed

½ (2 mL) teaspoon kosher salt (or salt to taste)

¼ cup (60 mL) olive oil

1 small head fennel (about 2 cups [500 mL]), shaved on a mandolin

6 fresh farmers' market radishes, slivered on a mandolin

¼ cup (60 mL) fennel fronds

The Chef ✤ Dana Ewart
Joy Road Catering, Penticton

The Farmer ✤ Jordan Marr
The Homestead Organic Farm, Summerland

Dana Ewart is one half of the superstar team of Joy Road Catering, and Cameron Smith is the other half. The highly sought-after cuisine created by this duo and their crew offer an incredible dining experience, featuring the exclusive taste of the Okanagan. They call it *cuisine du terroir,* which literally translates to "food of the earth," and it is a celebration of all things that come from our Okanagan soil. Joy Road caters and has also become famous for its Sunday night Alfresco dinners on glorious God's Mountain.

The two met and fell in love in Toronto in 1999, and their love affair with each other, and with food, blossomed from there. They moved to the Okanagan together in 2005, after travelling and cooking at various vénues.

Cam and Dana have their own little farm with pigs and chickens, but work closely with local farmers like Jordan Marr of the Homestead Organic Farm. Dana explains, "We have been working with Farmer Jordan for three years, and he's the best. We have an enormous amount of respect for him and are so lucky that he chose to farm—he could be doing anything else he put his terrific mind to. He has a blog called *The Ruminant* that peeps should check out. We meet every spring and talk about new interesting things that we would like to work with for the impending season or new things that he would like to try. We're pretty spoiled."

The two are always learning, travelling, eating, and exploring; they are a work in progress. In between travels, they live a hyper-local lifestyle. "Our love for food and for each other is pretty synonymous. We have always cooked together. The future of Joy Road? Pretty sure that Cam and I will cook together or for each other until we no longer can. Joy Road is the name of the road that we have our business/farm/home on—and it's the present incarnation of our lives together."

Jordan Marr and his wife, Vanessa, live on a farm in upper Summerland. Set on a gorgeous green plateau with stunning views beyond to Okanagan Lake, this land feels almost spiritual. Vanessa lives there part-time; the other half of her life is spent in Kelowna bringing babies into the world as a midwife.

Jordan explains how they came upon their farm life: "I got into farming by chance. I enrolled in an interdisciplinary program at UBC and was required to take a few courses on food security, food politics, and food production. I didn't grow up on a farm, but became interested in agriculture at that point, though more on the food/farming policy side. I met Vanessa in the same program. When we graduated, we decided to spend a season on a farm so we could see farming through the farmer's eyes. We liked the lifestyle, and decided that farming was the best way to be part of the growing movement to improve food security and bring more diversity to Canada's food system. In 2011 we moved to our current farm/home lease in the Okanagan and started our business. 2015 was our fifth season growing veggies here."

The future of farming in the Okanagan is bright, but one of the major obstacles for young farmers is land cost. Jordan explains, "My business is going well and I foresee lots of growth in demand for regionally produced farm goods. But I'm not sure if we'll be able to farm entirely on our own land. Currently we lease, which isn't bad, but we'd rather own. One idea is to buy a smaller piece of land, like an acre, where we could have a home, a nursery, and a couple of greenhouses, and then establish a few leases within a ten-minute drive. Having multiple leases at a time would buffer us against the inevitability of losing a lease when a landowner sells or changes their plans."

Joe and Jessica Klein are owners of the Homestead Organic Farm.

f /joy-road-catering 🐦 @joyroadcatering joyroadcatering.com

f /thehomesteadorganicfarm 🐦 @OKhomestead thehomesteadorganicfarm.ca

LEFT TO RIGHT: TYLER HARLTON, DANA EWART, VANESSA & JORDAN MARR

The Winemaker ✣ Tyler Harlton
TH Wines, Summerland

Growing up on a farm in Saskatchewan instilled a love of land and a strong work ethic in Tyler Harlton. After attending law school and pursuing other dreams, his heart brought him to Summerland in 2011 for a number of reasons, including his passion for farming and for wine. "What I've learned in Okanagan winemaking, especially as it pertains to my pursuit of a natural style," Tyler says, "is that our BC grapes are of exceptional quality and capable of pure expressions that set us apart from other wine regions in the world. It's inspiring to be a part of the Okanagan's artisanal community, one that extends beyond the food and wine crowd, comprising individuals that work hard to make authentic goods that tell the story of our place."

f /thwines   🐦 @th_wines   thwines.com

Pan-Roasted BC Scallops with Braised Radish, Sweet Corn & Cavolo Nero

 NAV DHILLON

 ROGER SLEIMAN

 CURTIS STONE

 NIKKI CALLAWAY

This gorgeous dish by Nav Dhillon of Old Vines Restaurant at the Quails' Gate Family Estate Winery in West Kelowna, features two relatively new rock star vegetables on the Okanagan farm scene: *cavolo nero* and fava greens. *Cavolo nero*, also known as black kale or Tuscan kale, is a kale variety that features long, slim leaves that are dark green to almost black. Fava greens are the leaves grown on the fava bean plant. They are mild flavoured and tender and delicious raw or cooked. Both of these vegetables are powerhouse vitamin greens.

Serves 2

Enjoy with 2013 Stewart Family Reserve Chardonnay, Quails' Gate Family Estate Winery

The nose opens with rich exotic spice, baked cinnamon pastries and butterscotch.

Opulent in the mouth, this wine has a creamy mouth feel with great fruit intensity and length.

Heat a medium-sized skillet on medium-high heat. Dress scallops with a spoon of vegetable oil and a pinch of salt. Add another 2 Tbsp (30 mL) of oil into the skillet, lay in the scallops flat side down, and sear until golden brown. After 45 seconds flip scallops over and add a knob of butter. Baste scallops for 30 seconds, finish with a fresh squeeze of lemon, and remove from pan.

Scrub radishes, removing any dirt, but do not peel. Heat vegetable stock in a pot with butter, thyme, and salt, and gently braise the radishes until cooked through. Shave one radish and set aside to garnish the dish.

Make nage: Boil a pot of salted water. Cook kale and fava greens for one minute, then strain, and submerge in ice bath for 2 minutes. Once cooled, blend the greens in a blender until smooth. To finish, add the butter to the blender and purée for 30 seconds.

Cut corn kernels off cobs. Juice half of the corn in a juicer and discard the pulp. Add juice to small saucepan and whisk the juice until it thickens over low heat. Season with a pinch of salt. Slowly roast the other half of the corn with butter in a skillet until the kernels turn colour and caramelize. Remove from heat.

To serve, spoon nage and corn onto a warm plate. Place braised and fresh radishes along with the scallops. Finish with trout roe and fava greens.

Scallops

6 fresh scallops

3 Tbsp (45 mL) vegetable oil

sea salt, to season

2 Tbsp (30 mL) butter

1 lemon

2 Tbsp (30 mL) BC Rainbow Trout roe (or to your liking)

Braised radishes

6 radishes, multicoloured plus one radish for garnish

1 cup (250 mL) vegetable stock

2 Tbsp (30 mL) butter

2 sprigs thyme

1 tsp (5 mL) sea salt

Nage

6 cups (1.5 L) *cavolo nero* (also known as black kale or Tuscan kale)

1 cup (250 mL) fava greens

1 Tbsp (15 mL) butter

fava greens, few stems to garnish

Sweet corn

4 cobs fresh corn

2 Tbsp (30 mL) butter

1 pinch sea salt

LEFT TO RIGHT: ROGER SLEIMAN, NAV DHILLON & CURTIS STONE

The Chef ✣ Nav Dhillon
The Culinary Director ✣ Roger Sleiman
Old Vines Restaurant at Quails' Gate Family Estate Winery, Kelowna

Born and raised in Vernon, Nav Dhillon cut her culinary teeth at the helm of some internationally acclaimed restaurants, starting with Gordon Ramsay's Maze in Melbourne, Australia. Upon her return to the Okanagan, she dove right into the winery restaurant culture, working as senior sous chef at Terrace Restaurant at Mission Hill Family Estate for a few years and honing her farm-to-table philosophy. Now chef de cuisine at Old Vines Restaurant, she has the opportunity to let her talents shine. Nav explains, "I work very closely with a few farmers in the valley and make the effort to go out weekly to the farms to see how

the produce is coming up. Tasting and seeing everything in the fields helps me get creative and inspires me for my next menu change. I have a lot of respect for our local farmers and the produce that comes in through the door. I believe in keeping the true flavors of the ingredients; without the quality of the product we get, that wouldn't be possible. I believe it is truly special to be able to enjoy our local wines with the grapes literally harvested at our doorstep and get produce from our farmers just minutes away. There are not many places in the world you can achieve that."

Roger Sleiman joined Quails' Gate Estate Winery in 2006 as winery chef and refocused the culinary program at Old Vines Restaurant with his basic cooking principles of keeping it simple, fresh, and local while staying true to the ingredients. In his new role outside of the kitchen, he oversees all of the culinary aspects of the winery and restaurant and says, "This is a very special place for me, and it is nice to see it evolve along with the Okanagan food movement."

f /quails-gate 🐦 @quails_gate quailsgate.com

The Farmer ✣ Curtis Stone
Green City Acres, Kelowna

Over the past few years, Curtis Stone has helped a new culture in the Okanagan skyrocket in popularity: urban farming. He has successfully demonstrated to those who are inspired to farm that it is possible to do so without owning any land.

Without enough land or capital to start his own growing operation, Curtis utilized an innovative strategy provided to him by the SPIN (Small Plot Intensive) program in the US, in which you "rent" garden space from homeowners. All produce is grown with natural methods, meaning no chemical fertilizers, sprays, or pesticides are used.

"In 2012, we grew over 50,000 lbs of food on less than an acre of land, using 100 percent-natural, organic methods and only 80 litres of gasoline," says Curtis describing his sustainable, innovative growing model. Green City Acres is mostly pedal-powered, meaning the majority of business, deliveries etc. are done on bicycles with custom-built trailers.

Curtis explains, "All I wanted to do was live by my values, and homesteading in a traditional sense, was the only way I could do that. But how does a guy who doesn't want to sign his life away to the bank for 30 years get a piece of property to farm on?

SPIN was the answer for me. First, I can grow all the fresh produce I need for my family and myself, thereby removing myself as best I can from the conventional system. And I can actually make a good living at it. I was sold. I would like to see young people who are disenfranchised with the 'system' to start a career in farming. I believe that if we want to change things for the better, we need to recreate the system ourselves. Protesting in the street does nothing. I think the future of urban farming in the Okanagan can be great, because we have an amazing growing climate, and we have thousands of huge lawns all over this city, just waiting to be turned up."

Curtis is now a published author. His book, *The Urban Farmer*, is a guide for start-up farms that want to follow his business model and sell to market. An educator and speaker, he has been travelling to events spreading the seed of inspiration, helping to form the next generation of farmers.

f /greencityacres 🐦 @greencityacres greencityacres.com

NIKKI CALLAWAY

farms over 180 acres of vineyards in the valley. Dick's son, Tony Stewart, is now in charge of the winery operations. Quails' Gate offers soaring views of Okanagan Lake as well as rich Okanagan history on the property. It has always been a mandate for the Stewart family to help preserve the heritage of the valley.

Senior winemaker Nikki Callaway trained in Bordeaux and spent time working in South Africa before coming to the Okanagan. The intimate nature, small-batch processing, and focus on quality at Quails' Gate are a perfect fit to her style and passion as a winemaker.

f /quails-gate 🐦 @quails_gate quailsgate.com

The Winemaker ⁜ Nikki Callaway
Quails' Gate Family Estate Winery, Kelowna

The Stewart Family is a pioneer in the Okanagan farming industry. Arriving in Kelowna in 1908, Richard Stewart Sr. founded one of the valley's most successful nursery businesses. About fifty years later, his son Dick Stewart decided to plant grapes.

In 1956, Dick purchased the Quails' Gate Estate land on the west side of Kelowna, and the first vines were planted in 1961. The Stewart family founded Quails' Gate Winery in 1989, and today the family

Brawn Terrine

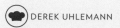 DEREK UHLEMANN

 GENE & SHELLY COVERT

 GENE COVERT

Terrines are gorgeous. From the rustic to the refined, terrine explains much about a chef's tastes and terroir. Like a pâté, a terrine is the vessel within which a forced meat (or vegetable) loaf is created. Very French, and sometimes challenging to create, a good terrine never fails to thrill. Chef Derek Uhlemann has created this mouthwatering terrine focusing on flavours Covert Farms—vegetables and wine—which will create a flavour unique to the Covert land.

Serves 8–12

Enjoy with 2012 Amicitia Red, Covert Farms Family Estate Winery

A blend of Cabernet Sauvignon, Cabernet Franc, Syrah, Petit Verdot, Malbec, Merlot and Zinfandel. Complex and well-balanced with notes of Black Forest cake, vanilla and wild berries following through with plums and spiced dark fruits on the palate.

Place water in a pot and add the salt and sugar. Bring to a low boil. When the salt is completely dissolved remove the pot from the heat and add the egg in its shell. If the egg floats, your brine is perfect! If the egg sinks and does not come back up add more salt. Repeat until the egg floats. Let the brine cool and pour into a non-reactive storage container.

Wash the pig head in cold water and scrub thoroughly. If the head is hairy, use a kitchen torch to remove the bristles and whiskers.

Place the pig head in the non-reactive container, and cover with brine to submerge. Weigh the head down with a plate or a large water-filled glass jar, and refrigerate overnight.

Remove the pig head in the morning and rinse well. Throw away the brine.

Place the pig head in a large stockpot and cover with water, add ½ the bottle of Pinot Blanc wine, Walla Walla onions, fennel, peppercorn, garlic cloves, bay leaves, cloves, and thyme bundle. Bring the liquid to a boil and then immediately reduce the heat and simmer for 4–6 hours or until the jaw detaches. While you are simmering, skim off and discard any grey foam that gathers on the top of the liquid. The more you discard impurities, the clearer your gel will be. To avoid cloudiness, do not stir or agitate the stock while it is cooking.

When the meat is tender and falling off the bone, remove the meat from the stock, and set aside to cool. Ready a fine mesh strainer and a smaller stockpot to collect the stock. Line the strainer with cheesecloth or a clean kitchen cloth and strain the stock into your new, smaller stockpot. Return the stock to the stove and reduce the liquid by one half on low heat. Taste for salt and adjust. Cool slightly.

Continued on page 90

Ingredients

33 cups (8 L) water

4 cups (1 L) coarse salt (or 1 cup per litre as needed, see egg method below)

2 cups (500 mL) cane sugar (or ½ cup cane sugar for every litre water)

1 egg

1 pig's head cleaned and washed (local suggestion: North Okanagan Game Meats)

1 bottle of Pinot Blanc (local suggestion: Covert Farms Family Estate Pinot Blanc), divided

2 organic Walla Walla onions, roughly chopped

4 ribs organic fennel bulb, roughly chopped

12 whole peppercorns

1 bulb organic garlic, peeled into cloves

8 bay leaves

6 cloves

1 bunch organic thyme, tied with string

¾ cup (190 mL) organic flat leaf parsley, finely chopped

sprigs from one organic fennel bulb, finely chopped

Continued from page 89

Drink a glass of the Pinot Blanc to prepare for peeling the tongue. Remove the tongue from the head and peel the outer skin off. It should peel easily. Remove the remaining meat from the head and chop or pull it apart to form a small dice. Chop everything—the ears, soft palate, and all the bits and pieces. The texture of the terrine is what makes it so tasty.

Gather a terrine mold or a bread pan and line with plastic wrap, allowing enough overhand so you have handles to remove your terrine when it has set. Mix all your meat in a bowl and combine in the mold pressing down firmly. Pour stock over the meat until it covers the meat entirely. If you don't have a terrine mold, soup bowls will also work well, and you can freeze them individually for later use.

Layer your finely chopped parsley and fennel over the liquid and wrap tightly making sure everything is covered and neat. Make sure your layer of herbs is ample and spread evenly. Refrigerate overnight. Unmold the cold terrine by grabbing your plastic handles and inverting it onto a plate or cutting board. Remove plastic, slice, and serve. Pour your final glass of Pinot Blanc.

Serve with an organic sourdough loaf and enjoy!

LEFT TO RIGHT: GENE COVERT & DEREK UHLEMANN

The Chef ❖ Derek Uhlemann
Covert Farms Organics, Oliver

Over the past few years, Derek Uhlemann has become so much more than the farm chef at Covert Farms Organics. He is now the winery operations manager, and has become intrinsically involved in the philosophy of the farm and farm livestock. He explains, "Our ethics are simply to support nature and not overwhelm it. We believe in minimal intervention in agriculture while supporting healthy food systems by creating organic soils using permaculture and having animals live in harmony with our vines and crops."

He and his wife, Sunny, were blessed with a little girl a couple of years ago, adding a wonderful new perspective to life—and, in particular, farm life. Derek explains: "Ruby Mae Poppy Uhlemann has changed our lives in our interaction with the animals of the farm. She has become friends with our chickens and Highland cattle and now demands that we see them when she visits. Having a child also makes us appreciate how close we are to our food in the Okanagan. I feel blessed that she will grow up in a community of wine and food makers."

The farm and winery has evolved and changed over the last couple of years, with the farm café/restaurant closing in order to focus on special events and farm dinners. This is where Derek's passion lies, and he says, "Our Farm Field Dinners were a big success this season. My favourite was the 'Oceans to the Okanagan' fundraiser for gravel restoration in the South Okanagan. We welcomed elders from the Okanagan National Alliance, Osoyoos Indian Band, Oceanwise, Slow Fish, and other partners to speak alongside chef Chris Whittaker of Forage and chef Jeff Van Geest of Miradoro. I am excited to continue this dinner in coming seasons with even more partners, and raise awareness of salmon habitat in the Okanagan."

f /covertfarmsorganics   🐦 @covertorganics   covertfarms.ca

The Farmers ❖ Gene & Shelly Covert
Covert Farms Organics, Oliver

Covert Farms is a 650-acre utopia of organic living in the Okanagan. Gene and Shelly Covert take pride in specializing in certified organic growing on their sprawling farm, which has every kind of vegetable you can imagine, berries, and an organic vineyard that feeds their Covert Farms Family Estate winery. It is also a salmon safe operation. In every way, the Coverts are conscious caretakers of this exceptional piece of nature.

Gene Covert is a third-generation farmer. He tended this land with his father and grandfather, who established it in 1959. Recently, Gene and Shelly have passed on the farming side of the business to focus on the wine, events, tours, and other aspects of the large operation. They say, "We have leased the organic produce to Secrest Organics run by Terry Grewal, a decades-long farm employee. We use the produce, along with our sensory garden, to provide a true farm-to-table experience with our farm field dinners and special events, which now includes weddings. We also offer farm charcuterie and cheese boards daily at the farm, which coincide with our signature experience farm tour: 'a culinary tour through Canada's desert.' We have increased our products to include value-added produce from the farm, including fermentation and canning, which is available on our farmers' boards and through our wine lounge. A big hit again this year was our dried smoked jalapeño peppers and lactic fermented pickles."

On the animal side to the farm: "We are now the proud owners of seven llamas who act as guardian animals to our Barbados Black Belly Sheep and our heritage chickens. We raised four Berkshire and five Mulefoot pigs this season, which have become two hams cured with gin aromatics from the local Dubh Glass Distillery, including yarrow, vanilla bean, orange peel, coriander, and juniper. We hope to work with Dubh Glass this coming year in creating a gin with organic botanicals foraged from the farm. We still raise our Highland cattle, which are an essential part of our biodynamic management of the fields and vineyards."

f /covertfarmsorganics   @covertorganics   covertfarms.ca

SHELLY & GENE WITH THEIR THREE CHILDREN

The Winemaker ❖ Gene Covert
Covert Farms Family Estate Winery, Oliver

"We craft wines with minimal intervention, using natural fermentation when possible to focus on vineyard and fruit. Our white wines display purity of fruit and a crisp natural acidity coveted by growers, and low yields result in terroir-focused artisan reds that are luscious and age-worthy," says Gene Covert. "Our focus on the farm has been directed to the winery and refining our approach to honest winemaking. Our new explorations have been in Methode ancestral sparkling wines and single varietal grand reserve wines. This year we received a silver medal from the San Francisco International Wine competition and a bronze medal from Decanter Wine Awards, 2015 World Wine, for our Amicitia and MDC blends."

f /covertfarmsorganics   @covertorganics   covertfarms.ca

A Short History of the Wine Industry in the Okanagan Valley

The history of winemaking in the Okanagan can trace its roots to the earliest European settlements near Kelowna. Father Charles Pandosy planted grape vines in 1860, but it was one of his hired hands, Giovanni Casorso, who began growing grapes on his new ranch across the creek from the mission in 1884. The varieties of both of these pioneering grape growers are lost in time. The Casorso family still owns the land today and produces wines for Sperling Vineyards.

By the early twentieth century, most of the large original Okanagan ranches had been sold off and subdivided into smaller properties for orchards or town sites. Eager new farmers experimented with crops to grow on their newly acquired land. W.J. Wilcox planted the first commercial vineyard in the interior in 1907 in Salmon Arm. Though the grapes were not grown for wine, Wilcox's vines supplied cuttings for the first large-scale Okanagan vineyards by J.W. Hughes in 1926. Hughes signed the first contract to grow grapes for a winery, Growers' Wines of Victoria. Two of Hughes' original vineyards are still in production today as Tantalus, St. Hubertus, and CedarCreek.

By 1932 a winery opened its doors in the Okanagan. Domestic Wines and Bi-products Ltd. began using local apples and then, in 1935, grapes to make wine. Later rebranded as Calona Wines, it was joined by Mission Hill and Casabello in the 1960s. This early era of BC's wine industry was based on producing large quantities of fruit using hybrid grapes and growing techniques designed to produce lots of fruit. Both grape growers and wineries needed the large volumes to be sustainable. The apogee of popularity in this era was the pop-wine trend in the 1970s with Baby Duck, Royal Red, and a flurry of faux-European wines.

In 1979, the provincial government created a new form of winery license based on small-scale productions observed in California. Gray Monk and Sumac Ridge were among the estate wineries from this first generation. The 1980s were hard for the new estate wineries. Higher-quality wines were a tough sell at prices that could make a profit. The Free Trade Agreement and the launch of the Vintner's Quality Alliance lit the fuse on the critical change that was needed to gain acceptance in the market and allow the creation of more estate wineries, which continues to this day.

LUKE WHITTALL

Luke Whittall is a wine professional working in the Okanagan Valley. He is currently writing a book (to be published in 2017) on the history of the wine industry in British Columbia.

MAINS

Green Croft Gardens Organic Corn & Chanterelle Pasta

 JEREMY TUCKER

 WOLF & GABRIELE WESLE

 ALEXIS MOORE

Green Croft Gardens is a delightful farm for chefs and food lovers to visit. Farmers, Wolf and Gaby Wesle are kind, hard working people who have created an oasis of certified organic farming. Happy animals roam the property, ranging from chickens, pigs, and sheep to horses and dogs, and almost every vegetable you can imagine prospers under their learned hands. Jeremy celebrates their organic corn in this unique and toothsome paste recipe.

Serves 3

Enjoy with 2014 Platinum Viognier, CedarCreek Estate Winery

Delightful tasting notes of honeysuckle on the nose, with ripe, fleshy apricot on the palate.

Remove the corn kernels from the cobs. Melt the butter in a large saucepan over medium heat until foaming; add shallots, garlic, and corn kernels. Sweat on medium heat, stirring occasionally for 6–7 minutes. Stir in cream and reduce heat to low. Simmer until the flavours have melded and the corn kernels are crisp but tender (not mushy) about 10–12 minutes.

Using a blender, purée the sauce in small batches until smooth. Strain the blended sauce through a fine mesh strainer to remove any solids. Season with salt and set aside.

Bring a large pot of water to a boil. Add pasta and kosher salt, and cook until al dente according to package directions. Drain.

In a large saucepan over medium-high heat, melt butter with olive oil. Add garlic and cook, stirring frequently, about 1 minute. Add chanterelles and tomatoes. Season with salt and pepper. Cook over medium high heat until tender, about 2–3 minutes. Taste and adjust for seasoning.

To serve: Reheat the corn sauce and ladle a bit into the bottom of each plate. Place a nest of pasta on top of the sauce. Finish with chanterelles and cherry tomatoes.

Enjoy!

Corn sauce

2 organic corn cobs

2 Tbsp (30 mL) butter

1 shallot, chopped

1 clove garlic, chopped

2½ cups (625 mL) heavy cream

1 tsp (5 mL) salt

Pasta

1 lb (2.2 kg) of your favourite pasta

1 Tbsp (15 mL) kosher salt

1 Tbsp (15 mL) unsalted butter

1 Tbsp (15 mL) extra virgin olive oil

1 clove garlic, thinly sliced

2 cups (1 pint) chanterelle mushrooms, cleaned, halved if large

1 cup (½ pint) heirloom tomatoes, chopped

freshly ground pepper and salt to taste

LEFT TO RIGHT: WOLF & GABRIELE WESLE & JEREMY TUCKER

always looking for the best and freshest products to offer my guests. It's not always about price. You do get what you pay for! Our local farmers are by no means getting rich. I think it's very important to know where your food comes from. It's very difficult to understand the challenges involved in growing exceptional food organically when you fill your shopping cart in the grocery store. Local may cost more, but without our support we may lose small local suppliers to the development of a growing city."

"You want to know why it's so expensive for that organic arugula? Maybe the farmer lost his early crop to hail, half of his next crop was targeted by pests and insects, or it's not as green because of unbalanced nitrogen levels—there are so many things that could wipe out a farmer's livelihood and we have no idea as we walk past mountains of produce at the grocery store.

"I am humbled every time I go to Green Croft Gardens. It's such an amazing place. Wolf and Gaby are two of the hardest working and caring people I know. They put a lot of love into their land and it really shows when you see their produce. They also have the cleanest produce at the market, just to show how much care and pride went into growing that ingredient."

f /cedarcreekwine 🐦 @cedarcreekwine cedarcreek.bc.ca

The Chef ❖ Jeremy Tucker
CedarCreek Estate Winery, Kelowna

The Farmers ❖ Wolf & Gabriele Wesle
Green Croft Gardens Certified Organic, Grindrod

Jeremy Tucker is dedicated to the Okanagan's local farming/artisan community and is an advocate for farmers. As executive chef at Terrace Restaurant at CedarCreek Estate Winery, he has the ability to source local producers as well as pair his food with award-winning wine. Originally from PEI where his life in the kitchen began as a teen, Jeremy's lifestyle now includes glorious summers in Kelowna and then majestic winters as executive chef at Snowwater Heli Skiing and Boarding, a boutique lodge in the mountains of Slocan.

On our precious farmers, he explains, "As a chef I'm

Wolf Wesle and his wife, Gabriele, own and operate Green Croft Gardens, a 20-acre certified organic farm in Grindrod bordering the Shuswap River. Originally from Germany, the family operates their farm according to Old World sustainability practice. They grow a wide range of delights, from berries and small fruits to beautiful organic vegetables, and they also have a wonderful assortment of farm animals that happily roam their land. Chickens, turkeys, sheep, cows, pigs, dogs, and horses all help create this "village" of goodness, which is quite close to being entirely self-sufficient.

Wolf started his career many years ago with a degree in agriculture from Germany and a background in dairy science. When he first moved to Canada, he worked in the dairy industry for 15 years before focusing on vegetable growing. The Wesle family bought its farm, now Green Croft Gardens, in 1988 and it is one of the earliest certified organic farms in the Okanagan.

Wolf and Gaby are both very involved in their community and the local farmers' market culture. Wolf has played in integral part in building and envisioning future plans for the Kelowna Farmers' and Crafters' Market and Gaby helps organize the Enderby Farmers' Market. It's all about community for them. Future plans include forming a farm co-op to connect local producers to local consumers, and to help local farmers band together to offer their goods in other markets.

The Wesles are very active in mentoring young farmers and encouraging future generations interested in organic farming. Their three children are also involved in the farm part-time as they pursue other interests, with daughter Jennifer now playing a larger role.

The amount of labour involved in organic growing, weed management, and the planning required for soil management to sustain an organic farming status for the long-term is incredible. Many young men could not handle the workload that Wolf does. They work hard, but they love what they do—it is their calling, their passion, and you can see it in their smiles.

f /green.c.gardens   greencroftgardens.com

ALEXIS MOORE

recognition and accolades for its Pinot Noir. The terroir in Kelowna's upper Lakeshore Road region provides ideal conditions for more Burgundian-style wines.

Winemaker Alexis Moore completed her degree in viticulture and oenoleogy at the prestigious Lincoln University in New Zealand, and her experience ranges from the vineyards of Provence to Sonoma and Oregon's Penner-Ash Wine Cellars. Before joining the CedarCreek team, she was in Burgundy, France, rounding out her knowledge of the heartbreak grape and both Old World and New World winemaking technique and philosophy.

f /cedarcreekwine   ✎ @cedarcreekwine   cedarcreek.bc.ca

The Winemaker ✣ Alexis Moore
CedarCreek Estate Winery, Kelowna

Originally purchased in 1986 by the Fitzpatrick family, CedarCreek released its first wines in 1987 and was one of the eight pioneering wineries of BC. In 2014, Anthony Von Mandl (of Mission Hill Estate Winery) purchased the winery with a plan to continue the legacy and brand of CedarCreek. The range of its portfolio remains, and it has been receiving huge

Sterling Springs Stuffed Chicken Thigh Wrapped in Wild Boar Bacon with Crispy Chicken Chorizo, Creamed Corn Purée & Pan-Seared Pine Mushrooms

JAY BENNETT

LISA & HANS DUECK

ANDREW STONE & TERRY MEYER STONE

A little more effort goes into creating this dish, but it is worth it. Traditionally, a ballotine is a deboned thigh/leg of the chicken, duck, or other poultry that is stuffed with ground meat and other ingredients. It is tied with twine to hold its shape when cooked, or is sometimes stitched up with a trussing needle. Have fun!

Serves 6

Enjoy with 2013 Wildfire Pinot Noir, Anarchist Mountain Vineyard

"Very lifted, fragrant cherry, cinnamon, herbal and floral aromas are compelling. It's medium weight, open-knit, juicy, and nicely focused."—David Lawrasen

Make the corn purée: cook the corn in butter with shallots, garlic, salt, and pepper for 3 to 5 minutes. Pour into blender and purée on high speed for 3 minutes, adding the cream slowly. Set aside for serving.

Make the chicken forcemeat. In a food processor combine the chicken thigh, cream, egg white, thyme, roasted garlic, sautéed shallots, salt, and pepper and purée for 2 to 3 minutes. Cover and refrigerate until ready to make the ballotine.

Make the ballotine. Place the bacon side by side on several layers of cling wrap. Spread a thin layer of the chicken forcemeat on the bacon leaving a ¾-inch (2-cm) border free of forcemeat. Place chicken thighs skin side down throughout the centre of the bacon. Spoon out chicken purée into the middle of the thigh and, using the cling wrap, gently but firmly roll the bacon over the chicken thighs to enclose the forcemeat into the centre (like a sushi roll). Tie the ends tightly with butcher twine, making sure the ballotine is well wrapped. Bring chicken stock to a simmer, add chicken ballotine and poach for about 2 hours (don't boil; try to keep a light simmer).

Let cool in the stock for 2 hours and then refrigerate for up to 6 hours. Take out of cling film and sear in a frying pan until bacon is crispy.

Warm up the corn purée. Drain most of the bacon fat from the frying pan and then fry the chorizo and pan-sear pine mushrooms.

Slice the ballotine into 1-inch (2.5-cm) thick pieces and serve atop the corn purée with the chorizo and pine mushrooms scattered around. A masterpiece! Enjoy.

Creamed corn purée

3 cobs sweet corn, kernels cut off
2 Tbsp (30 mL) butter
2 shallots, finely chopped
2 cloves garlic, finely chopped
salt and pepper
⅛ cup (30 mL) heavy cream

Chicken forcemeat

1 boneless chicken thigh, cubed
¼ cup (60 mL) cream
1 egg white
pinch thyme, finely chopped
2 cloves garlic, roasted
2 shallots, sautéed
⅛ tsp (0.5 mL) salt
⅛ tsp (0.5 mL) pepper

Ballotine

6 boneless chicken thighs
10 pieces boar bacon, sliced
8–12 cups (2–3 L) chicken stock
1 link of Sterling Springs chicken chorizo (cut into thin strips)
5–6 small pine mushrooms

JOHANNA, DEB THE CHICKEN, LISA, JACOB, MARIA THE CHICKEN, HANS DUECK & JAY BENNETT

The Chef ❖ Jay Bennett
Ranch Cafe, Falkland

In 2012, chef Jay Bennett and his wife, Sarah, decided it was time to leave the city life and move back to his hometown of Falkland, BC. He grew up in the kitchen of his mother's restaurant, the Ranch Cafe, a landmark on the main strip of tiny Falkland and a hub for the community; this is where his passion for cooking was ignited. As a youth, Jay says he was inspired by his grandma's amazing cooking and he "strongly believes he acquired his great taste from her while growing up and eating her home cooking."

Jay is self-taught and explains that he had a "short but career-changing experience" at Canoe restaurant and Spencer's on the Waterfront in Ontario. As he honed his cooking philosophy, he realized that "what I wanted to do simply couldn't happen in a city," referring to the ability to not only access ingredients from farmers and artisans who live down the road, but also to be able to participate in farming. Jay explains, "Being in Falkland and in the Okanagan, is one of the best places in the world for a chef. There is great opportunity here. Moving forward, I want to have everything on the menu made from scratch with everything locally sourced." In 2014 he officially took over operations at the Ranch Cafe, and the menu is in transition. It has retained its diner favourites, which locals have come to rely on after 24 years, but Sarah has taken over the baking role and is adding her talents to the menu, and Jay is integrating his new farm-to-table dishes.

Jay is proud to have partnered with farmers Hans and Lisa Dueck at Sterling Springs Chicken, who are also neighbours in Falkland. Jay says, "So many of the great dishes I create start with the great products from my selected farmers."

f /pizzaranchcafe

The Chicken Farmers ❖ Lisa and Hans Dueck
Sterling Springs Chicken, Falkland

Lisa and Hans Dueck present a wonderful model of a family farming business based on Old World ethics and sustainable farming techniques. "One of our favourite things about our farm is that our whole family can work together," explains Lisa. "Our kids, Johanna (13) and Jacob (11) are involved in the day-to-day activities on the farm, including hatching, chores, deliveries, farmers' markets, etc. We homeschool both kids because we want them to be able to participate in the whole experience of running the farm and setting up a business—the hard work involved, the successes, the stresses, and everything that goes along with developing a growing business. We're all learning and working together, and it's been a wonderful opportunity to share this experience with our kids. It's rewarding and humbling to be able to provide families with an amazing product, and the support and encouragement we've received has been overwhelming."

Originally in the commercial chicken farming industry, Hans is now able to follow what he knows is best for his birds: a proper diet, and clean, comfortable pens that allow his chickens to live stress-free, which is key for not only an ethical farming practice but also to offer the most tender and delicious meat to customers.

"One of the exciting new developments on our farm has been the introduction of an on-farm hatching program. Our goal was to ensure a medication-free product from egg to customer. It's an incredible experience to see these tiny chicks hatching before our eyes!"

Instead of going the mass production route, which is stressful on the birds, Lisa explains, "Another step forward for us has been the development of a small network of backyard farmers who help to supply our business with chickens. We firmly believe that there should be opportunity for people to return to the small, family-run concept of farming. Growing a small number of birds helps to ensure that the chickens receive the care and attention they need, and makes it

TERRY MEYER STONE & ANDREW STONE

easier to produce a top-quality product. We are thrilled to be able to partner with a number of families to help them realize their desire to farm on a part-time basis. It's a team effort!"

f /sterlingspringschicken   sterlingspringschicken.com

The Winemakers ❖ Andrew Stone & Terry Meyer-Stone
Anarchist Mountain Vineyard, Osoyoos

Andrew Stone and Terry Meyer-Stone dove headlong into the vineyard life directly from a busy life in city. Neither knew much about wine except that they loved to drink it. Then, while they were "testing out" the wine life by living on Terry's brother Jak's Okanagan Falls vineyard, they fell in love with a vineyard atop Anarchist Mountain in Osoyoos.

They started out by growing and selling the vineyard's grapes, which were coveted by many of the region's top winemakers, before deciding to try their hands at their own wine label. And thus, Anarchist Mountain Vineyard Chardonnay and Pinot Noir were born, with both receiving much acclaim.

Terry and I (Jennifer Schell) are also partners in Garagiste North Small Guys Wine Festivals featuring the under-2,000 case producers (visit our website at garagistenorth.com). The *London Financial Times* rated our concept festival as one of the top 5 in the world in 2015!

f /anarchistvineyard   🐦 @anarchywines   anarchistvineyard.com

Cedar-Roasted Chicken with Spruce & Sumac

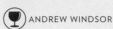

JEFF VAN GEEST

STEVE & ANDREA GUNNER

ANDREW WINDSOR

Chef Jeff Van Geest of Miradoro Restaurant in Oliver made this incredible chicken dish when he was a guest chef at one of my Food/Wine/Farm Workshops at Okanagan College. The aromas of roasted chicken and cedar boughs is unique and makes your mouth water. Serve the chicken atop fresh cedar for a fabulous, festive presentation. And yes, we are talking about the cedar shrubs in your backyard, as long as they're completely organic and pesticide-free. Sumac also grows locally; ask your farmer.

Serves 4

Enjoy with 2014 Oldfield Series 2 Bench White, Tinhorn Creek Vineyards

Notes of passion fruit, white and yellow flowers, white peach and a subtle smokiness greet your nose. The palate is at first bright and zesty with passion fruit and lime, but as the wine builds it shows fresh apricot and nectarine notes, before finishing with lime freshness again.

Preheat oven to 425°F (220°C). Season chicken inside and out with salt and pepper.

From the backside of the chicken, slide a finger under the skin over each of the breasts to separate the skin from the breast, and slide a tablespoon of butter over each breast under the skin. Stuff the cavity with garlic, lemon, and cedar, and then truss the chicken with butcher's twine to hold the wings and legs into the body. Place cedar boughs in a roasting pan and place the chicken on the cedar. Sprinkle the sumac on the chicken and place in the oven. Immediately lower the temperature to 350°F (180°C). Roast for about 45 minutes (depending on the size of the bird), until juices run clear when you pierce the bird between the leg and the body. Turn up the oven to 450°F (230°C) and brown the skin of the bird until crispy and dark golden in colour. Remove from oven and let rest in a warm spot for 20 minutes before serving.

1 whole Rosebank Farms chicken

kosher salt and fresh-cracked black pepper, to taste

2 Tbsp (30 mL) butter

4 cloves of garlic, cracked lightly with the side of a knife or the heel of your hand

1 lemon, cut into quarters

organic cedar boughs, enough to line a roasting pan and a few for stuffing the bird (toast with a torch before using)

sumac, enough to liberally sprinkle over the outside of the chicken

butcher's twine

JEFF VAN GEEST

STEVE AND ANDREA GUNNER

The Chef ✤ Jeff Van Geest
Miradoro Restaurant, Oliver

Born and raised in St. Catharines, Ontario, Jeff Van Geest hit the Vancouver culinary scene first as an apprentice and then a sous chef at the iconic Bishop's Restaurant—a pioneer in sustainable, seasonal farm-to-table cuisine. A pioneer in his own right, Jeff went on to open his own restaurant, Aurora Bistro, in Vancouver. It had an innovative wine list; Van Geest only offered BC wines alongside his raved about, locally focused cuisine.

Growing up with farmers as grandparents, Jeff developed his respect for fresh local produce at a very early age. "I was drawn to the Okanagan by the natural beauty, the wine, the proximity to the farmers, the escape from the city, and the house prices," says Jeff. Now able to raise his young family near fishing lakes (this guy loves to fish!) smack in the middle of South Okanagan wine country, the guy is certainly in his element.

"My favourite ingredient is whatever is seasonal and coming in the back door of the kitchen; however, if I had to choose one, I would say peaches. I have a very strong childhood memory of eating warm, ripe peaches right off the tree in Southern Ontario. Eating good peaches now always brings me back to those times (like that scene in *Ratatouille*). I'm excited to be able to essentially be working 'next door' to the farmers that supply me the local ingredients on the menu."

Van Geest is an amazing teacher and has been sharing his knowledge and passion for his art and philosophies at Okanagan College as well as doing private classes at Miradoro Restaurant, where he has been executive chef since 2010. He is authentic, true to his locavorian brand and his support of local producers. He lives and breathes it, and has become an integral part of the movement that is taking the Okanagan culinary scene to greatness.

f /miradororestaurant ✖ @miradororesto miradoro.ca

The Chicken Farmers ✤ Steve & Andrea Gunner
Rosebank Farms, Armstrong

Steve Gunner came from a farming background, previously operating his own mushroom farm in Langley. Andrea Gunner grew up with two classical musicians as parents but found her passion in horticulture, in which she completed a B.Sc. degree with a minor in agricultural economics. The two met and fell in love on the mushroom farm.

In 1994, Steve and Andrea purchased a seven-acre farm in Armstrong and began their joint career in agriculture where they would eventually specialize in raising sustainably farmed poultry. Andrea explains, "We focus on raising happy, healthy chickens and turkeys in a pasture system without the use of antibiotics, animal by-products, or GMOs. We feed freshly milled organic grains from start to finish and supplement the baby chicks in the brooder with sprouted grains, pulses, and oilseeds. After years of raising chickens and turkeys using intensive rotational pasture grazing systems, and seeing the almost miraculous improvements resulting from soil tilth, organic matter, and decreasing noxious weed populations, we have expanded operations onto satellite farms in an effort to help young or new producers develop profitable farms and rehabilitate their depleted and/or mismanaged soils. This arrangement has allowed us to supply more poultry while controlling the feed, supervising the animal welfare, and providing an income for young or new producers. We established our own feed mill in partnership with one of our young satellite farmers in 2013, and have since added more grain storage bins and upgrades to the milling facility. This provides fresh feed each week, which is really beneficial, keeping feed costs down through less waste."

The Gunners are big picture people, and through their passion and support of the farmers, they see growth in our very flawed local meat industry. "With our customer's continued support, we are working hard to rebuild the local agricultural economy. When

ANDREW WINDSOR

you buy pastured meat, you're not only taking a step to safeguard your health, protect the environment, and improve animal well-being, you're also supporting sustainable farming and the farmers who choose to practice it. Small, local family farmers are invaluable members of rural communities and play a key role as stewards of the land."

f /rosebankfarms 🐦 @gunnerarosa rosebankfarms.ca

The Winemaker ✤ Andrew Windsor
Tinhorn Creek Vineyards, Oliver

Tinhorn Creek Vineyards is legendary for its sustainability practice and super-green operating methods. Owners Ken and Sandra Oldfield (the original winemaker) continually strive to improve their efficient, earth-friendly winegrowing operation. Known as the "Compost Queen," Sandra Oldfield has become a role model for other Okanagan vineyards looking to adopt a policy to reduce their carbon footprint. The Oldfield's are green machines who are creating award-winning wines the earth-friendly way.

Winemaker Andrew Windsor, whose goal is to "make amazing wine (and have an awesome time doing it)," joined the team in 2014 after working at wineries in France, New Zealand, and Niagara.

f /tinhorncreek 🐦 @tinhorncreek tinhorn.com

Moroccan-Spiced Vale Farms Lamb Leg with Roasted Pumpkin Romesco, Chanterelle Mushrooms & Leek Hay

 ROB CORDONIER

 CHARLOTTE RUECHEL

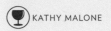 KATHY MALONE

Chefs are basically food artists and chef Rob Cordonier has beautifully created this succulent lamb dish as a visual memory of his visit to Vale Farms. The bucolic and colourful farmscape made an impression in his mind. Green rolling hills, a garden full of pumpkins, bushes of orange sea buckthorn berries, fields dotted with sheep, and hay bales in cozy barns all contribute to his elegant and delicious portrait of an autumn farm in the Okanagan.

Serves 6–8

Enjoy with 2013 Syrah, Hillside Winery

The 2013 Syrah opens with black raspberry and notes of clove and espresso, which interweave with black currant and a touch of cardamom on the palate. Elegant fine-grained tannins lead into a powerful juicy finish.

Preheat your oven to 375°F (190°C). Combine the diced pumpkin, onion, garlic, almonds, hazelnuts, cinnamon, nutmeg, salt, cayenne, thyme, and 3 Tbsp (45 mL) of olive oil in a mixing bowl and toss well. Place on a baking sheet and roast the pumpkin mix for 15 minutes uncovered to begin caramelization. Cover the vegetables with foil and cook for another 15 minutes to steam so that the pumpkin is completely soft. Combine the pumpkin mix with the rest of the ingredients in a blender and purée on high speed until very smooth. Serve immediately or cool and store in the fridge until needed. This can be made ahead and will hold in the fridge for a week.

Lamb: Debone the leg of lamb and cut away any cartilage or connective tissue. Mix the seasonings and massage into the meat. Marinate the lamb leg for 24 hours in the refrigerator. Remove from fridge and roll and tie the roast into a tight bundle with butcher's twine. Preheat oven to 400°F (200°C). Roast the lamb leg for 10 minutes then reduce the oven temperature to 315°F (160°C) and roast for 30 minutes or until the centre of the roast reads 125°F (51°C) on a meat thermometer. Remove the roast from the oven and lightly cover with aluminum foil. Rest the lamb for 10 minutes before serving. While the roast is resting, heat the pumpkin romesco and hold over low heat.

Continued on page 112

Pumpkin romesco sauce

1 lb (500 g) sugar pumpkin, large dice
½ cup (125 mL) white onion, sliced
3 Tbsp (45 mL) garlic, sliced
3 Tbsp (45 mL) almonds, blanched
3 Tbsp (45 mL) hazelnuts, peeled
1 tsp (5 mL) ground cinnamon
½ tsp (2.5 mL) nutmeg, freshly grated
1 tsp (5 mL) salt
¼ tsp (1 mL) cayenne pepper
1 Tbsp (15 mL) thyme leaves
3 Tbsp (45 mL) olive oil
2 Tbsp (30 mL) maple syrup
½ cup (125 mL) olive oil
⅓ cup (75 mL) sea buckthorn juice (or orange juice)
½ cup (125 mL) water
pinch saffron

Lamb

2.5 lb (1.25 kg) boneless lamb leg
3 Tbsp (45 mL) Ras el Hanout spice (a Moroccan spice blend)
1 tsp (5 mL) saffron
zest of one orange
3 bay leaves
3 Tbsp (45 mL) red onion, diced
4 Tbsp (60mL) fresh ginger, minced
1.5 tsp (7 mL) salt
⅓ cup (75 mL) olive oil

Continued from page 111

Prepare the leek hay ahead of time. Trim away the root and the green leafy top of the leek. Cut the stalk in half and clean any dirt from between the layers. Cut into long thin matchstick size (or "julienne"). Toss the leeks in cornstarch and deep fry at 280°F (138°C) following the directions of your deep fryer. When the bubbles have stopped (approximately 45 seconds), the leeks should be nice and crisp but still green in color; remove the leek hay from the deep fryer and drain on a paper towel to remove excess oil. Lightly season with sea salt and hold until needed.

Mushrooms: Heat a large skillet over high heat and add the oil and butter. When the butter starts to foam, add the chanterelles and sauté for 3 minutes or until lightly browned. Season the mushrooms with salt and pepper as desired and sprinkle with the thyme.

To serve: Spread the pumpkin romesco onto a warm serving dish. Slice the rested lamb leg and place in the middle of the dish. Arrange the chanterelles around the roast. Scatter the mint and orange zest over the plate. Place the leek hay in a stack on top of the lamb. Sprinkle your favourite finishing salt lightly over the whole dish and serve immediately—following a toast to Vale Farms, of course!

Leek hay

1 leek, julienned

1 Tbsp (15 mL) cornstarch

pinch fine sea salt

2 Tbsp (30 mL) mint
  leaves, for serving

zest from 1 orange, for serving

Mushrooms

2 Tbsp (30 mL) grapeseed oil

2 Tbsp (30 mL) butter

4 cups (300 g) chanterelle
  mushrooms

sea salt, to taste

pepper, to taste

2 tsp (10 mL) thyme leaves

LEFT TO RIGHT: ROB CORDONIER, SHAUN, LAMBERT, CHARLOTTE RUECHEL

The Chef ✤ Rob Cordonier

Fire & Fife Consulting and Catering, Penticton

After spending many years at the helm of the Hillside Winery Bistro, Rob Cordonier is striking out on his own in creating his new consulting and catering company. Says Rob, "I will be doing custom catering for groups of up to 30 people. My diverse background in the culinary industry will allow me to create menus and events specific to a customer desires. I am also providing kitchen consulting to help companies/restaurants update their menus and cost them properly to maximize profits. I am studying right now to include kitchen and restaurant design to my repertoire of expertise."

Rob Cordonier was known for enthusiastically pairing wines from Hillside Estate with the bounty of the Okanagan fields in the Hillside Bistro. He says, "The food and the wine brought me here, but it is the contagious passion of the people who are a part of the food and beverage scene here in the Okanagan that have made this such a rich experience to be a part of as a chef."

Rob has thoughtfully created this roasted lamb dish in honour of Vale Farms. He explains, "I wanted to convey the sights, textures, surroundings, and obviously ingredients, from my most recent visit to the farm in this dish. I really wanted to try to capture the essence of that morning at the farm. I hope people can recreate the dish and imagine themselves there."

"I wanted to be partnered with Vale Farms in this book," he ardently explains, "because they are really farming in a way that respects the natural needs of their livestock. The sheep are pasture-fed in a natural environment, and I think they are the happiest, healthiest, tastiest lambs I have ever come across."

Rob and his wife, Melissa, became parents recently, with son, Everett, now enriching their lives. "Becoming a father has enhanced how I value the region in regards to quality of life, and the quality people who we are lucky to have as neighbours and friends that contribute to our food, drink, and agriculture. I will share as much of the Okanagan culture as I can with my son, and hope that he learns to appreciate the subtlety that one's endeavors can provide to a meal, drink, and life. There is an incredible richness in this valley that can only be measured one bite, sip, and smile at a time."

250-486-1902

The Farmer ✤ Charlotte Ruechel

Vale Farms, Lumby

Vale Farms offers an idyllic farm scene, the kind you would imagine as a child: red barns; cows, calves, sheep, and lambs grazing in the green pastures; chickens pecking around; animals to pet; and a friendly, smiling farmer. The farm was created through many years of hard work, which included some heartache for the Ruechel family. Charlotte Ruechel explains, "My husband Michael and I studied agricultural sciences in Germany dreaming about farming one day. To make this dream come true, we immigrated to Canada in 1975 and bought this beautiful piece of land. In 2001, the farm became organic. Unfortunately, my husband had a serious riding accident in 1991, which left him severely brain injured. We have been taking care of him in our home for the last 24 years. Now the next generation, our two daughters and their husbands, have taken over the production of our grass-fed beef and lamb, and pasture-raised turkey, chicken, and pork."

The farm has a shop where locals can buy direct and Charlotte also attends the Kelowna Farmers' and Crafters' Market in their Vale Farms trailer, offering their beautiful organic meats as well as sea buckthorn juice, a superstar health berry the Ruechels grow on the farm.

Charlotte continues, "We always had the dream of sharing this beautiful land with others in a way that also brings an understanding of farming and food production to the next generation. My daughter Emily and her husband, Don Hladych, decided that a Waldorf-inspired school on the farm would make this possible through creating an intimate connection between the school's curriculum and the seasonal farm events. To see the children come over on a very regular basis to witness and sometimes help with the farm work is very exciting." (To learn more about Cedar Bridge School, visit cedarbridgeschool.com.)

"We love the challenges of farming without chemicals. We love the dairy, which supplies us with valuable compost/manure for soil improvement, we love the fact that we can supply a nice variety of healthy proteins to our community, and, most of all, we love seeing the animals live their lifecycle in the most natural and free way possible. I also really love interacting with our customers directly at the market. That completes the cycle in a most rewarding way."

valefarms.com

The Winemaker ❖ Kathy Malone

Hillside Winery and Bistro, Naramata

Winemaker Kathy Malone has been a strong member of the Okanagan wine community for over 30 years. She was part of the Mission Hill Winery team when

KATHY MALONE

in 2008 she made the move to the Naramata Bench. Since then, she has studied the unique terroir of the area and tailored her winemaking style to best express the estate's vines in small lots. She explains, "By respecting and showcasing the fruit of these vines, I want to give our wine drinkers the chance to share in the discovery and development of this special region."

Kathy works closely with Brent Pillon, the executive chef at the winery Bistro, finding the "soul of each wine" for him to build his menu around and creating perfect food and wine pairings.

f /hillsidewines   🐦 @hillsidewines   hillsidewinery.ca

Pan-Roasted Arctic Char with Braised Beluga Lentils & Smoked Heirloom Tomato-Peach Gastrique

CHRIS VAN HOOYDONK

GARY KLASSEN

BERTUS ALBERTYN

Fresh, tender, and flavourful, Road 17 Arctic Char is pristine from gentle handling and almost zero shipping time. Beluga lentils are actually just pulses, little black lentils that are named for their glamorous lookalikes—beluga caviar.

Serves 6

Enjoy with 2014 Origin White Blend, Maverick Estate Winery

Fresh and lively nose with a floral scent, some apple, lime and hint of lemongrass complete a complex and interesting aroma. Refined palate with intense tropical fruit and mineral flavours is completed with a fresh and zesty natural acidity.

Quarter heirloom tomatoes, place in a smoker on cold smoke for approximately 15 minutes (light smoke). Remove and cool.

Heat olive oil in a medium saucepan on medium heat. Add shallot, garlic, and peaches and sauté for 5 minutes or until shallots become translucent. Add wine and honey. Simmer until wine is almost dry. Add tomatoes and lemon juice and bring to a simmer. Once tomatoes break down, set aside to cool and add herbs and spices. When cool, purée in blender until smooth, season to taste with salt and pepper and strain. Serve at room temperature.

Lentils: Heat olive oil in a medium saucepan on medium heat, and sauté vegetables and garlic with smoked paprika until tender (approximately 5 minutes). Deglaze the pan with wine, stir, and continue to cook until the wine has disappeared. Add lentils, stir to coat with residual oil, add stock, and bring to a simmer. Cover and cook at low simmer until lentils are tender, approximately 30–40 minutes. Set aside to cool.

Fish: Rinse fish and pat dry with a paper towel. Lightly "score" the skin to allow for even crisping. Season the flesh side with salt and pepper, if desired.

Heat a non-stick frying pan on medium heat. Add oil and place fish skin side down (do not crowd pieces, depending on number of pieces—it's best to do in different batches). Cook until skin is crisp and golden brown in color, then flip in pan, and add butter and a slice of lemon. Cook as desired; it is best served medium.

To serve: Mound half a cup (125 mL) of beluga lentils on each plate, top with fish, and drizzle with gastrique.

Smoked heirloom tomato-peach gastrique

6 large heirloom tomatoes, quartered
2 Tbsp (30 mL) olive oil
2 shallots, peeled & sliced
1 clove garlic, minced
2 whole peaches, pitted and sliced
½ cup (125 mL) white wine
2 Tbsp (30 mL) honey
2 Tbsp (30 mL) lemon juice
1 sprig each lemon verbena, lemon balm, tarragon
8–10 leaves basil
½ tsp (2.5 mL) curry powder
¼ tsp (1 mL) smoked paprika
salt and pepper, to taste

Braised beluga lentils

2 Tbsp (30 mL) olive oil
½ onion, finely diced
1 carrot, finely diced
1 yellow or orange sweet bell pepper, finely diced
½ cup (125 mL) corn kernels
1 clove garlic, minced
1 tsp (5 mL) smoked paprika
½ cup (125 mL) white wine
2 cups (500 mL) beluga lentils
4 cups (1 L) stock (chicken, vegetable, or duck)
salt and pepper

Arctic char

6 6-oz (170-g) pieces of Road 17 Arctic Char, skin-on
1 Tbsp (15 mL) organic canola oil or grapeseed oil
1 Tbsp butter
slice of lemon
salt and pepper

LEFT TO RIGHT: GARY KLASSEN, CHRIS VAN HOOYDONK & HIS APPRENTICE, KYLE CAMPBELL

The Chef ✤ Chris Van Hooydonk
Backyard Farm Chef's Table, Oliver

After years of working in a restaurant environment, including a stint as executive chef at Burrowing Owl Winery's Sonora Room, Chris Van Hooydonk decided it was time to follow his dream and build Backyard Farm Chef's Table, his own cooking school/catering headquarters. Van Hooydonk reflects: "This project was motivated by my desire to find a better balance between the most important parts of my life. Our business now has allowed me to be better farmer, husband, father, and mentor, essentially while working from home."

The stars aligned and a perfect property came available in Oliver with two homes, one to live in and one to convert into the kitchen/chef's table, and grounds that included gardens and fruit trees—the perfect package! After an ambitious year of renovating, Chris, his wife Mikkel, and family opened Backyard Farm Chef's Table in June 2014 and welcomed their first guests.

"The food program and my culinary philosophies at Backyard Farm are inspired by a great many things surrounding us in the South Okanagan. The menu planning is always a reflection of seasonal produce availability, either from our two acres of organic-practice orchard and raised-bed garden property, or the harvest of our dedicated and passionate farmers and producers. In addition, a priority is made to represent the wealth of quality wines located throughout our region. The opportunity to educate our guests about the importance of supporting our local farmers, tourism partners, wineries, and region as a whole has been at the forefront of our vision."

Backyard Farm happens to be just up the road from the Klassen's fish farm. Chris says, "I am a huge fan of Road 17 Arctic Char for many reasons! I am firm in my philosophy of sustainability; this fish is not only Ocean Wise certified, but all natural, and hormone and antibiotic free."

f /chris.hooydonk 🐦 @hooydonk_van backyard-farm.ca

The Fish Farmer ✤ Gary Klassen
Road 17 Arctic Char, Oliver

Fish farms have received a bad rap in the past due to irresponsible farm placement, which ended up wreaking havoc on our ocean environment. The Klassen family however, is the good kind of fish farmer, using innovative, environmentally friendly farming techniques in an enclosed land facility. As owner/fish farmer Gary Klassen explains, "Our fish do not come from a limited source, we are not depleting wild fish stocks. We clean our water to mitigate the risk of adverse effects on the environment."

You may wonder how they could be raising coldwater fish in the desert landscape of Oliver? Gary came upon the idea of farming the coldwater fish by chance. He explains, "We moved from the Peace River region of Alberta. We bought the farm as a cleanup project and fell in love with the property and area. We drilled a well for geothermal heating and discovered a consistent 12°C (54°F) temperature. We tested the water and found it offered the perfect conditions for arctic char."

The Klassens raise the arctic char from eggs, taking two years before the fish mature. The fish are raised and housed in an 8,000-square-foot concrete building known as "the barn," which draws cold water from a pathogen-free aquifer on site. They operate without hormones, antibiotics, vaccines, or any medications. The facility utilizes state-of-the-art systems to ensure consistent water quality and temperatures.

Gary does have a farming background, but nothing akin to what he is doing now! He says, "I was born and raised on a farm, we raised cattle, hogs, chickens, and grew grain and forage grass seed. I operated a metal fabrication company initially to fund our farm startup." This is a family farm operation, just as Gary had envisioned. Son Layne is a fishery technologist and the resident computer guru in charge of production, management, and ensuring consistent, top-quality fish. Daughter Brittany specializes in

LEFT TO RIGHT: BERTUS & ELZAAN ALBERTYN (WITH THEIR TWO DAUGHTERS), SCHALK & LYNN DE WITT

intensive fish care and really "loves the little fish," she establishes their feeding schedules and looks out for their well-being.

🐦 @road17char   road17char.ca

The Winemaker ✤ Bertus Albertyn
Maverick Estate Winery, Oliver

Schalk de Witt immigrated to Canada with his wife, Lynn, and daughter, Elzaan, in 1990 from South Africa with the dream of purchasing a vineyard and making wine. Years passed before something serendipitous happened: Elzaan fell in love with and married one of her childhood friends, a South African winemaker named Bertus Albertyn. Bertus also had a dream to come to Canada and make wine. And so it was to be. This new family, with its shared passion for wine, purchased Maverick Estate Winery. Their first vintage in 2011 received much acclaim.

f /maverickwinery   🐦 @maverickwinery   maverickwine.ca

Sockeye Salmon Tacos Two Ways

ROSS DERRICK

JON & ANN-MARIE CROFTS

DAVE GOKIERT

Fish tacos are one of my favourite foods, as are fish and chips at chef Ross Derrick's the Table at Codfathers Market in Kelowna. One bite into a fish taco and I am blasted straight back into summer mode—this is a dish that will get me through the long Okanagan winter. Ross has offered two ways to prepare the salmon taco: one ceviche style and one deep-fried until it's crispy. Enjoy!

Serves 2

Enjoy with Tree Brewing Kelowna Pilsner

The clean, crisp taste of the traditional European Pilsner is complemented by just the slightest taste of hops.

Ceviche salmon taco: Combine the lemon, lime, pineapple juice, shallots, garlic, and chilies in a bowl. It is best to leave this overnight, as the flavour will vastly improve. Strain so only the juice remains before adding the fish. When ready to eat, add the salmon and let sit for 30 minutes in the liquid. Strain and serve (assembly instructions at bottom of method).

Crispy salmon taco: Ross uses gluten-free flour made by Nextjen Gluten-Free, a wonderful company in Vancouver run by the husband-and-wife team of Hamid Salimian and Jennifer Peters. I now use it at home and, as promised, it makes for a crispier crust.

For dredging: Combine the dry ingredients. Add the vinegar and water and mix well. Allow to sit for 3 minutes. Dredge the salmon pieces in flour and dip into batter.

Fry pieces of salmon in oil set at 350°F (180°C) for about 3 minutes, or until it is nicely coloured and the pieces float to the top of the oil. Remove and drain on paper towel.

Pico de Gallo sauce: Combine all the ingredients, and let sit for an hour to allow flavours to marry.

To serve both versions: Shred some nice lettuce. Place on tortillas, top with a piece of the ceviche salmon or a piece of the deep-fried fish. For the crispy salmon taco, finish with a drizzle of Pico de Gallo sauce.

Garnish both versions with cut limes, crème fraîche, and cilantro.

For both tacos

2 pieces (1 lb [250 g]) fresh salmon, cut into ½-inch (1-cm) dice

Ceviche salmon taco

1 piece lemon, juice and zest
2 pieces lime, juice and zest
3 Tbsp (45 mL) pineapple juice
½ shallot, sliced
1 clove garlic, sliced
½ red Thai chili, chopped, seeds removed pinch salt

For dredging crispy salmon

¾ cup (190 mL) cornstarch
¼ cup (60 mL) flour (Nextjen if you have it) + 1 cup (250 mL) for dredging
1 tsp (5 mL) baking powder
pinch salt
splash cider vinegar
½ cup (125 mL) sparkling water, plus extra if necessary

For serving both versions

shredded lettuce
tortillas
cut lime wedges, for garnish
crème fraîche or sour cream, for garnish
chopped cilantro, for garnish

Pico de Gallo sauce

3 large tomatoes, cut into ¼-inch (6-mm) dice
1/red onion, finely diced
3 cloves garlic, grated fine on a microplane
2 limes, zested
2 Tbsp (30 mL) lime juice
1 bunch cilantro
salt to taste

LEFT TO RIGHT: JON & ANNE-MARIE CROFTS, ROSS DERRICK

The Chef ❖ Ross Derrick
The Table at Codfathers Market, Kelowna

Talking to chef Ross Derrick, you will usually hear him bring up a couple of topics. First is his little girl, Audrey. A dedicated single father, he is doing such a wonderful job raising her. Next, his other love: food.

Ross knew he wanted to become a chef in Grade 5. He owes the inspiration to Marlene Pfeffer, a caterer in his neighbourhood who owned a kosher catering company called Prepared Pleasures. Ross trained at the esteemed Stratford Chefs School in Ontario, a school that has offered the Okanagan a few celebrated chefs. The school is unique in that it has always focused on farm-to-table cooking and building community. From there, he followed his dream to move to Ireland and work as pastry chef at Cafe Paradiso.

After a couple of big career moves in the Okanagan (a stint at Sparkling Hills and then a job as executive chef at the Delta Grand Okanagan Resort), he realized that he wanted his own place more than ever. Chatting over dinner one night with Codfathers Seafood Market owner Jon Crofts, he learned that a space in the fish shop was coming available. Miraculously, the Table at Codfathers opened just three months later (thanks, Ross says, to the multitude of friends who chipped in their labour to make it happen). "I wanted to create a business that focused on sustainability, and Ocean Wise is very important to me," he says. And that is exactly what he built—complete with roommates like Codfathers next door, the business represents the pinnacle of sustainable seafood.

f /thetableatcodfathersmarket 🐦 @thetableseafood   thetableatcodfathers.com

The Fishmongers ❖ Jon & Anne-Marie Crofts
Codfathers Seafood Market, Kelowna

When it comes to fishmongers, you will not meet more community-minded and earth-minded ones than the Crofts. Jon has won many community awards, including some through the Okanagan Chefs Association, which praises him for his charity contributions and for providing a topnotch product they can trust. He also has a unique relationship with the local ONA (Okanagan Nation Alliance)—the first nations fishery managing the sockeye salmon's natural migratory routes and allowing the fish to run back into our local waters—helping them with promotions and support.

Jon is also quite a card with wonderful British wit. He explains, "I became a fishmonger after my mum issued an ultimatum: get a job and pay me rent or else! The first job I applied for was for a management trainee in an up-market fresh food company called Waitrose in the UK, and one of the first areas that I was assigned to was the new fishmongers program. I soon began to realize that my heart was not in management and that I loved dealing with the beautiful products that we received daily from the coast. I remember the distinct fresh smell of each product, the amazing colours, and the stunning exotic fish that arrived weekly from the Seychelles. I also loved learning the different textures and flavours, which I had never been exposed to before. After my mediocre management career, when we emigrated to Canada, I finally got my chance to run my own fishmonger's shop."

After purchasing the shop, Jon and Anne-Marie had a lot of work to do to transform it into a properly sustainable business operation. He says, "Sustainability is, for me, an absolute requirement as I could not look in the mirror each morning if I thought I was squandering my children's resources for the future. Ethical trading is to me about enjoying the relationship I have with my fishers and producers, and it is good karma, because if you look after people, when you need them, they will look after you too."

For more information on the sockeye salmon and the amazing work of the ONA's fisheries projects, visit syilx.org.

f /CodfathersSeafood   @thecodfathers   codfathersseafoodmarket.com

DAVE GOKIERT

The Beer Maker ✤ Dave Gokiert
Tree Brewing Co., Kelowna , Tree Brewing Institute

Tree Brewing has been making its award-winning handcrafted beer in Kelowna since 1996. Brewmaster Dave Gokiert and his team of passionate brewers use 100 percent malted barley, the finest hops, yeast, and water, and their concoctions are sure to satisfy the most discriminating tastes.

Taking the craft beer revolution to another level, Tree opened up the Tree Brewing Beer Institute in 2015, offering beer lovers a place to taste, learn, and hang out.

These happy hoppers give back too through their charity, the Community Pint Program. Fifty cents from every pint sold at the Beer Institute on Tuesdays will be donated to a local charity or organization.

f /treebeer   @treebrewing   treebeer.com

f /treebrewingbeerinstitute   treebrewingbeerinstitute.com

Cheffrey's Wild Boar Ragu

GEOFFREY COUPER

RICHARD YNTEMA

HOWARD SOON

This delicious pasta recipe is the quintessence of Tuscan-style slow food. Like chef Geoffrey Couper (affectionately known as Cheffrey) of Okanagan College in Kelowna, the dish is rich with personality and bursting with charm. It is best served around a big table with friends and family.

Serves 8–10

Enjoy with 2012 Small Lots Barbera, Sandhill Wines

Master Winemaker Howard Soon has finely crafted Canada's only Barbera in its classic style, offering full ripe flavours and smooth tannins with moderate acidity.

The day before you make the ragu, bring the red wine and the mulled wine spices to a simmer over medium heat on the stove. Take off the heat and let steep for 10 minutes. Strain and cool the flavoured wine, then add the red wine vinegar. Marinate the diced wild boar shoulder overnight in this liquid.

The following day, drain the meat in a colander, reserving the marinade for later. Lay the meat on a tray lined with 2–3 layers of paper towel. Place two more layers of paper towel on top to dry off the meat and bring to room temperature. Preheat the oven to 250°F (120°C).

In an 8-litre ovenproof pot, render the diced pancetta over medium heat until the fat has melted. Remove the pancetta and reserve. Lightly season the diced boar with salt and freshly ground black pepper, then brown the meat over medium-high heat in the pancetta fat in 3–4 small batches, adding more olive oil as needed.

Once all the meat has been browned, add the finely diced onion, carrot, and celery to the pot and lightly caramelize. Add the garlic and chili flakes and cook until fragrant. Stir in the tomato paste and continue cooking, stirring occasionally, for 2–3 minutes. Add the seared boar meat and pancetta back to the pot, then stir in the reserved marinade, canned tomatoes, and beef stock and bring to a simmer. Cover the pot and place in the pre-heated oven for approximately 3½–4 hours, or until the boar meat is fork-tender. Adjust the final seasoning and pair the ragu with your favourite fresh pasta, gnocchi, or polenta.

*Note that any braised or stewed dish is best served after it has "rested." If time permits, safely cool down the ragu and then reheat and serve it the next day! And in Cheffrey speak, "Et voila!"

---

2 cups (500 mL) red wine

2 Tbsp (30 mL) mulled wine spice blend

¼ cup (60 mL) red wine vinegar

3½ lbs (1.5 kg) boneless wild boar shoulder, diced into ½-inch (1-cm) pieces

3½ oz (100 g) pancetta, finely diced

salt

freshly ground black pepper

½ cup (125 mL) olive oil, or as needed

4 cups onion, finely diced

2 cups (500 mL) carrot, finely diced

2 cups (500 mL) celery, finely diced

1 Tbsp (30 mL) garlic finely, chopped

2 tsp (10 mL) red chili flakes

⅔ cup (160 mL) tomato paste

1 28-oz (796-mL) can diced tomatoes

2 cups (500 mL) beef stock

GEOFFREY COUPER WITH OKANAGAN COLLEGE CULINARY ARTS CLASS OF 2016

The Chef ❖ Geoffrey Couper
Okanagan College Culinary Arts Program, Kelowna

Past chairman and president of the Okanagan Chefs Association, culinary apprenticeship instructor, wine lover, and raconteur extraordinaire are just a few of the toques that Geoffrey Couper, or "Cheffrey," wears. With three decades of award-winning experience behind him, his obsession with great food, prepared simply with passionately produced local products, only burns brighter. Having called Kelowna home for over 10 years, he has had the opportunity to provide culinary inspiration for many great wine producers in the valley, including Mission Hill, CedarCreek, Blue Mountain, and Andrew Peller among others.

A chef on the run, Geoffrey has boundless energy that he shares with his lovely wife, Michelle, three children (and two dogs). He is active in all areas of his life—the ski hill beckons whenever possible. In the past, Geoffrey has been a private chef at exclusive heli-skiing resorts.

Geoffrey says about teaching, "The process of learning about food and cooking is really the start of understanding so much about our world and ourselves."

His advice to all young chefs looking for education and inspiration? "Go work on a farm." After a classic apprenticeship, Geoffrey departed for Europe to do the typical travel, eat, and work thing, thinking he knew a fair bit about cooking. He ended up on a small family farm in southern Germany, and what the young culinarian soon realized was that, while he may have known about cooking, he knew nothing about food. And there is a huge difference between the two. He says, "To see products destined for the table being raised, weeded, milked, vinified, to witness firsthand the tremendous effort it takes to produce great food, will undoubtedly make a huge impact on the way any young cook views their profession."

He is fun, tells wonderful stories of his adventures and anecdotes during his lectures, and exudes such a passion for his craft. This is one special teacher, and the community adores him.

He says, "Food is everything. It is life and death, history and culture. It is love and hate, memory and celebration. Wealth and poverty, chemistry and romance—the list is truly endless."

f /okanagancollege 🐦 @okanagancollege okanagan.bc.ca

RICHARD YNTEMA

HOWARD SOON

The Farmer Butcher ✤ Richard Yntema
North Okanagan Game Meats, Enderby

Located in beautiful Enderby, Richard Yntema's farm and abattoir are an important part of our industry's livestock production and an example of what the future of processing should look like.

A house builder by trade, Richard left his home in Abbotsford 22 years ago with his family to come to the Okanagan and buy a farm.

Richard's focus is raising and sourcing hard-to-find products for chefs across the valley. He raises wild boar, deer, lamb, and chickens and sources other meats like rabbit, veal, and exotic poultry.

In 2008, the government changed the licensing requirements for processing meat privately. This new law forced farmers to transport livestock as far as the coast to a processing plant. This process was financially hard on the farmer and on the animal. Richard made a major investment in his operation and became a provincially licensed processing plant. He is now able to butcher his own livestock, and that of others, on the farm.

The farm is very much a part of our culinary education culture. Ethical chefs, as well as the Culinary Arts Department at Okanagan College (e.g., Geoffrey Couper), bring their teams and students for farm tours and to view the animal processing. Richard says the best chefs understand the "connection to the animal and where the meat comes from." He also offers the peace of mind that the animals enjoyed "a good life on his farm." The wild boar roam freely in a mini forest area and the deer frolic in a beautiful pasture. Richard has set a high standard for animal farming as well as running a green operation. The entire operation is run on geothermal heating and cooling systems, making his carbon footprint zero.

250-838-7980

The Winemaker ✤ Howard Soon
Sandhill Wines, Kelowna

Howard Soon is a celebrity in the Canadian wine world and a true pioneer in the industry. He is a kind man, well loved and respected for his craft. Howard has also been generous in sharing his vast knowledge in wine making and viticulture, and has mentored and nurtured many talents over the years.

Howard joined Sandhill Wines in 1997 and has created a special portfolio of small-lot wines that represent his best winemaking efforts. He was the first winemaker in BC to release a series of single-vineyard wines. "Our Small Lots Program provides a glimpse into our wine-making future, capturing the essence of small batches of promising new varietals."

Howard became the first winemaker in history to receive all three top honours for Sandhill Wines at the 2009 Wine Access Canadian Wine Awards, winning Best Red Wine of the Year, Best White Wine of the Year, and Winery of the Year.

f /sandhillwines   🐦 @sandhillwines   sandhillwines.ca

Deer Sliders with Green Tomato Jam

BRIAN FOWKE

BONFIRE CULINARY
GARDEN

BILL EGGERT

Deer or venison is a local commodity that hopefully more food lovers will begin to appreciate. Wild meats are highly nutritious and regulated hunting is really a form of foraging that we should embrace. This is a party-size menu and chef Brian Fowke of Bonfire Restaurant in Kelowna has included recipes for all the fixins as well. Feel free to adjust to half or quarter, but the patties do freeze nicely, so one big batch will make for easy access to last-minute dinners and get-togethers.

Makes 26 big 8-oz (225-g) burgers or 60 sliders

Enjoy with 2011 The Bear, Fairview Cellars

Cabernet Sauvignon is the foundation of this wine, comprising 60% with Merlot, next at 25%, Cabernet Franc at 12%, and Malbec at 3%. Look for light red fruit on the front palate with the Merlot providing a lush full mid-palate and the Cabernet Sauvignon providing dark fruit overtones that continue on the finish.

Make deer burgers. Wrap the crackers in a kitchen cloth and smash to a fine crumb. Add the parsley, mustard, and minced meat to the bowl. Crack in the egg and add a good pinch of salt and pepper. With clean hands, scrunch and mix everything up well. Do not over-mix.

Mould each piece into a roundish shape, about 3 oz (90 g) each. Drizzle the burgers with oil, put on a baking sheet, cover, and place in the cooler.

Day one: In large covered container, stir together water and salt until salt dissolves. Add cucumbers; cover and refrigerate overnight.

Day two: in a stockpot, stir together jalapenos, vinegar, sugar, celery seeds, turmeric, and mustard seeds. Bring to a boil. Drain cucumbers from salt water; add cucumbers to saucepot. Return mixture to a boil; remove from heat. Let cool, then transfer to a covered container, and refrigerate until chilled

Chipotle: Mix all ingredients together and set aside.

Pickles: Mix all the ingredients together in a bowl and serve alongside burger. Party on!

24 cream crackers
8 sprigs of fresh flat-leaf
   parsley
¾ cup (190 mL) Dijon mustard
1 lb (500 g) ground pork
11 lb (5 kg) ground deer meat
4 large free-range eggs
sea salt to taste
freshly ground black pepper
olive oil

Chipotle aioli
4 cups (1 L) mayonnaise
3 Tbsp (45 mL) chives,
   finely chopped
4 cloves garlic, minced
4 Tbsp (60 mL) lime juice
1 Tbsp (15 mL) canned
   chipotle, chopped finely
   with adobo sauce
pinch sea salt and pepper

Bread and butter pickles
5 cups (1.25 L) cold water
5 Tbsp (75 mL) kosher salt
4 pickling cucumbers, sliced
   ⅛-inch (3 mm) thick
3 jalapeno peppers, sliced
   ¼-inch (6-mm) thick
1½ cups (375 mL) apple
   cider vinegar
1½ cups (375 mL) sugar
1½ tsp (7.5 mL) celery seeds
1½ tsp (7.5 mL) ground
   turmeric
1½ tsp (7.5 mL) yellow
   mustard seeds

Pickle coleslaw
1 jalapeno pepper, thinly sliced
1 head green cabbage,
   thinly sliced
4 large carrots, julienned
1 small red onion, thinly sliced
¼ cup (60 mL) bread-and-
   butter pickles, julienned +
   3 Tbsp (45 mL) pickle juice
1 cup (250 mL) mayonnaise

BRIAN FOWKE

The Chef ✤ Brian Fowke
Bonfire Restaurant, Kelowna

New to the Okanagan, chef Fowke spent a large part of his career leading the kitchen at Vancouver's legendary Joe Fortes Seafood and Chop House. No stranger to the Okanagan, Brian has done many road trips over the years to the valley sourcing products, meeting farmers, and choosing wines. When the opportunity to take over the helm at the Bonfire Restaurant came about, he scheduled a visit and tour; after seeing the culinary garden that his predecessor, chef Grant de Montreuil, and his wife created, Brian says, "I took the job on the spot."

Brian has redesigned the menus and culinary program for Bonfire and The Cove Lakeside Resort, and is excited to dive into the garden next year. Because of the size and diversity of the culinary garden, which has 25 different crops, Brian is planning to celebrate it to the max—by season and by ingredient. Stay tuned for garden festival dinners and events. In the meantime, he will be touring around meeting new farmers, tasting wines, and "breathing in the life of the Okanagan."

f /bonfirerestaurant 🐦 @bonfire_cove bonfirerestaurant.ca

The Farmer ✤ Brian Fowke
Bonfire Culinary Garden, Kelowna

The formidable Bonfire Culinary Garden is located beside the Bonfire Restaurant and it is not your average restaurant garden—it is half an acre in size! Chef Fowke will be taking over the operations of the garden with a farmer team. Plans are for seasonal celebrations and festivals, tours, and setting up a public market for locals and guests of the resort. There will also be laying hens on the team to provide fresh eggs for the restaurant. The goal is to demonstrate a true farm-to-table menu that allows guests to experience the garden up close, tasting and smelling the ingredients just as the chef does.

bonfirerestaurant.ca

The Winemaker ❖ Bill Eggert
Fairview Cellars, Oliver

BILL EGGERT

Known as the "Cab Man," Bill Eggert creates high-quality Cabernet-based wines at his winery up in the hills of Oliver. On his six-acre vineyard, Bill grows premium Cabernet Sauvignon on one half of the land and Merlot and Cabernet Franc on the other. A row of Syrah and Petit Verdot are also on site with some Sauvignon Blanc, his only white wine. Many of the names of his wines have a very interesting story attached. Two Hoots is named for the two little owls that patrol his vineyard. Bill's 2009 The Wrath wine is a heavenly creation and its epic name is appropriate. Not only because of its divine depth and rich palette of flavours, but also because of bizarre weather conditions that contributed to its making. One side of Bill's Cabernet Sauvignon vines was virtually destroyed by hail—it was brutally battered by Mother Nature. Bill's first thought was to let the grapes hang and ignore the mess; his second thought was *What the hell?* He salvaged the clusters that had some skins and pulp still intact as well as any untouched bunches that had been protected from the wind-blown hail. He pressed. He waited. He tasted. The result was a concentrated, rich wine, similar to Italy's famous Amarone wines made from semi-dried grapes.

Bill can be found around the vineyard (he is a *vigneron*, a grape grower and winemaker), or in the rustic cabin on the estate that acts as his tasting room. If you are lucky, he will play you a tune on the piano while you taste.

f /bill.eggert 🐦 @fairviewcellars fairviewcellars.ca

Wild Moon Organics Berkshire Pork Meatballs in Tomato Sauce

MARK FILATOW

RICHARD QUIRING

PASCAL MADEVON

Leave it to chef Mark Filatow of Waterfront Wines Restaurant in Kelowna to transform the humble meatball into a gorgeous, gourmet experience without making it difficult. One of his tricks? He always uses the very best ingredients, locally sourced, of course. Wild Moon Organics pork is incredible. Mark and I visited Richard Quiring on the farm and met all of the happy piggies living there.

Makes 32 meatballs

Enjoy with 2013 R&D Blend, Culmina Estate Winery

This Merlot, Cabernet Sauvignon, and Cabernet Franc blend shows enticing aromas of ripe red cherries, cedar, and sweet spices. Subsequent random sampling reveals a rich, full-bodied wine with juicy blackberry flavours and a subtle vanilla taste.

In a stand-up Kitchen Aid Mixer outfitted with the paddle attachment, place the pork and all the spices (not the wine). Mix on medium speed for approximately one minute.

Lower the speed and add the wine while it is running. Then, turn the mixer to a high speed and let it run for one minute. The mixture should look a little shiny and sticky. Use the mixture to form 32 round meatballs and place on a tray. (The meatballs can be refrigerated until ready to use. It is best to make and cook them in the same day.)

In a skillet on medium-high heat, sear the meatballs, maybe 10 at a time. Don't worry about browning them. Once lightly seared, place in a pot large enough to hold all of them with the tomato sauce. Repeat with the remaining meatballs. Once all the meatballs are seared add the splash of red wine to the still-hot skillet, and scrape up all the brown bitties. Pour this into the pot with the meatballs.

Add the tomato sauce to the pot. Place on a medium-to-low heat. Bring the mixture up slowly to a light simmer, lightly stirring every two minutes. Then, turn the heat off. Check a meatball for doneness; it should have no pink left. If the meatball is a little pink, place the pot back on a low heat for two minutes. Taste the sauce; adjust for salt if need be. Enjoy ladled over your favourite pasta. Chef Filatow likes Garganelli. Shave some good sharp cheese over it and serve.

Meatballs

2 lbs (1 kg) Wild Moon Organics Ground Berkshire pork (keep cold)

2 tsp (10 mL) sea salt

1½ tsp (7.5 mL) ground black pepper

2 Tbsp (30 mL) dried oregano

1 Tbsp (15 mL) paprika

1 Tbsp (15 mL) fennel seed, coarsely ground (mortar and pestle works great)

2 cloves of garlic, minced

100 mL red wine

4 cups (1 L) really good tomato sauce (preferably homemade; Filatow uses Cascade tomatoes from Stoney Paradise)

salt

sharp cheese, shaved for serving

His dedication to local farmers and artisans is palpable and he is as humble as he is successful. You will see him at the early morning farmers' markets shopping for this restaurant and warmly chatting with his farm friends. He is the real deal and walks—and bikes—the talk. Mark is an extremely earth-friendly human and lives a sustainable lifestyle. He and his young family are active in the community and very athletic. Mark was an early participant in the Growing Chefs program, which sees chefs entering classrooms to teach kids about food, and is a generous contributor to various charities.

I am honoured that he wrote the foreword to this book. His dedication to his local cooking philosophies, consistent excellence, and ethics are to be applauded. Mark's respect for food can be summed up in one telling comment: "Something that I say to all who work with me: it is our job not to ruin this carrot on its way to the plate."

f /waterfront-wines-restaurant-wine-bar 🐦 @wfwines waterfrontrestaurant.ca

LEFT TO RIGHT: RICHARD QUIRING & MARK FILATOW

The Chef ✣ Mark Filatow
Waterfront Wines Restaurant, Kelowna

Mark Filatow is executive chef, sommelier, and partner at Kelowna's celebrated Waterfront Wines restaurant and Details Catering. Mark's impressive resumé includes Tofino's Wickaninnish Inn, Vancouver restaurants Bishops and Diva at the Met, and Kelowna's Fresco Restaurant (now RauDZ Regional Table). He was named Top Foodie Under 40 by *Western Living* magazine, has won the BC Gold Medal Chefs competition, and has cooked at the prestigious James Beard Foundation House (and the list goes on). In 2001, he became one of the only chefs in Canada to be accepted into the prestigious Sommelier Guild.

The Farmer ✤ Richard Quiring
Wild Moon Organics, Armstrong

Richard Quiring's Armstrong farm is built around catering to the comfort and stress-free lifestyle of its residents, the Berkshire pigs. Richard has a history in pig husbandry, and this time around, he is using all of his past learnings combined with a dedication to ethical farming. There are very few pig farmers left in the Okanagan, making Richard's product even more desirable. He says, "Organic pork is hard to come by as almost all pigs are fed a diet of grains that are grown conventionally, with a heavy emphasis on the use of chemicals and commercial fertilizers. While only using organic ingredients costs significantly more to raise our pigs, we feel so much better about the quality and health of the meat as a result. Commercial pork is like a totally different meat category in contrast to the organic, pastured, heritage-breed pork that we supply. We are committed to raising our pigs in a stress-free environment for their entire lives, primarily out of respect for the animals that we care for. Interestingly, this has a dramatic impact on the quality of the meat that is produced. Nutritious and healthy pastures, space to wander and explore, comfortable shelters, and the very best in nutrition leads to an amazing meat quality."

The pastures are beautifully green in a bucolic setting, exactly what you would hope to imagine for farm animals. Says Richard, "I love working in the pastures with the pigs and just observing them enjoying their surroundings—they make me smile, regardless of how other things might be affecting me! My greatest satisfaction, however, comes from the interactions with our customers—the constant appreciation they express for what we do and the pork that we supply is incredibly motivating. It is also a true blessing to be able to do what I do alongside my son, Tristan." Eldest daughter, Joleah, is an herbalist and has also become involved with the farm, developing an amazingly nutritious and tasty bone broth.

In his twenties, Richard pioneered alternative housing developments and management systems for pig production, moving the animals into semi outdoor, large group buildings bedded with straw. His more humane methods of farming changed the way many family farms raised pigs across Canada and the USA.

f /thewildmoonorganicsco   wildmoon.org

LEFT TO RIGHT: ELAINE, SARA, & DON TRIGGS, WITH WINERY DOG BARRY.

Opened in 2013, Culmina is gracefully perched atop the hillside of the Golden Mile in Oliver, with vineyards circling and rising up to what is the highest-altitude vineyard in the South Okanagan. The Chardonnay grows up there, on Margaret's Bench, at 595 metres elevation. Pascal Madevon is creating the wines at Culmina, in the vineyard and cellar. He is a classically trained French viticulturalist and celebrated winemaker.

f /culminawinery   @culminawinery   culmina.ca

The Winemaker ❖ Pascal Madevon
Culmina Estate Winery, Oliver

Everyone in the wine industry knows the last name Triggs. Don Triggs and his partner, Alan Jackson, singlehandedly put the Okanagan wine world on the map with their first winery: powerhouse brand Jackson-Triggs. After leaving the business in 2006, Don and his family (wife Elaine and daughter, Sara), have returned to the wine scene, sending shockwaves of excitement through the grapevines. This new venture has been thoughtfully in the works since 2007.

Milk-Braised Pork Jowl with Apricot-Viognier Glaze & Nectarine Mostarda with Kale

 ROB WALKER

 BOYD & JOAN COLLINS

 ALISON MOYES

This beautiful dish by Rob Walker of Liquidity Bistro in Okanagan Falls is a celebration of the Okanagan's beautiful stone fruits. The glaze can be used alone on any cut of pork, as can the mostarda, making this dish very flexible.

Serves 4

Enjoy with 2014 Viognier, Liquidity Wines

This fuller-bodied wine has rich aromas of peach, dried apricot, honey and melon, with a sumptuous mouthfeel and flavours of ripe juicy apricot, citrus, peach, and a hint of white pepper, with a zippy finish.

Place all ingredients into a medium-size saucepan and stir together until mixture is well incorporated. Cook over medium-low heat for 45 minutes, stirring frequently.

Check the seasoning. Place into a blender or food processor and pulse 3 to 4 times, the mostarda should be textured and not completely smooth. Cool and reserve to serve with pork jowl or use an accompaniment to your favourite meat and poultry dishes or with some charcuterie.

Apricots: Quarter the apricots, remove stones, but leave the skins on. Pour the wine and water over the sugar in a large saucepan and bring to a boil to dissolve to syrup, this will take 4 to 5 minutes. Add the quartered apricots, lemon juice and orange zest, bring to a boil, and cook uncovered, skimming off any impurities that form on the surface. Cook the mixture for 20 to 25 minutes on low heat. Place the apricots and all the liquid into a blender. On the lowest speed, pulse, then purée until smooth. Cool the glaze. (This recipe is great for canning too! Just add to hot jars and seal.)

Pork: Preheat oven to 325°F (160°C). Place pork in ovenproof roasting pot with the rest of the ingredients. Cover pot and place in the oven for 2½ to 3 hours until pork is fork-tender.

Chef's note: I like to cool the pork in the braising liquid if it's not being served immediately. When serving, remove pork from liquid and pat dry.

Turn oven up to 400°F (200°C). Heat 1 Tbsp (15 mL) of oil in a sauté pan over medium-high heat; sear one side of the pork until golden and caramelized. Flip the pork over and liberally brush on the apricot glaze. Place the pork back in the oven for 8 to 10 minutes. To serve, you can slice the meat thin or evenly cut into 4 portions and serve with nectarine mostarda.

Nectarine mostarda (makes 2L)

2 lbs (1 kg) fresh nectarines, stones removed
1 cup (250 mL) of water
½ cup (125 mL) white wine vinegar
1 cup (250 mL) of sugar
2 tbsp (30 mL) black mustard seeds
¼ cup (60 mL) grainy Dijon mustard
¼ cup (60 mL) yellow mustard
2 tbsp (30 mL) smoky paprika
1 tsp (5 mL) kosher salt

Apricot-viognier glaze (makes 2L)

2½ pounds (1.25 kg) apricots
½ cup (125 mL) Liquidity Viognier (or other white wine)
½ cup (125 mL) water
4 cups (1 L) sugar
2 Tbsp (30 mL) lemon juice
2 strips orange zest

Milk-braised pork jowl

1½–2 lb (1 kg) fresh pork jowl, trimmed and cleaned (substitute a fresh pork belly if jowl is not available)
1 Tbsp (15 mL) olive oil
2 sprigs sage
2 sprigs rosemary
1 bay leave
5 cloves garlic, peeled
½ white onion, sliced
½ cup (125 mL) Liquidity Viognier wine (or your favourite white wine)
1 teaspoon (5 mL) sugar
1½ cups (375 mL) whole milk
¼ cup (60 mL) heavy cream
kosher salt and coarse ground black pepper

LEFT TO RIGHT: ALISON MOYES, ROB WALKER, BOYD & JOAN COLLINS

The Chef ✤ Rob Walker
Liquidity Bistro, Okanagan Falls

Chef Rob Walker joined Vintage Hospitality, a restaurant development and management company focused on the South Okanagan wine region, to open the Bistro at Liquidity. Vintage Hospitality also currently operates the Sonora Room Restaurant at Burrowing Owl Estate Winery and the Gunbarrel Saloon at Apex ski resort. He describes the best thing about his current digs as "getting to work with really professional, passionate people like my bistro staff, our winery staff, and my suppliers. I also have the opportunity to cook good, fresh, seasonal food for the most amazing guests that I have ever had the pleasure to cook for, making this place very special to me. And, the view from my kitchen is by far the best in the valley!"

Rob graduated from the culinary program at Okanagan College in 2001 and went on to exciting achievements in the culinary arts, including two gold medals in the Western Canadian Culinary Arts Festival and honourable mentions in both the BC Place Food Service Expo 2005 and the EAT! Vancouver CityTV Master Chef Competition 2005. He also has sommelier training, making his current work as a winery chef the perfect pairing.

Rob is focused on creating a menu spotlighting the local producers and the taste of the local Okanagan Falls terroir. He explains his relationship with his suppliers: "I truly think of them as part of my team and as my friends; they take care of me and I take care of them." Rob's method is "pairing the dish around the wines," making each menu item a celebration of the marriage between food and wine. And what does Okanagan Falls terroir taste like? Rob says, "OK Falls terroir, for me, tastes like our wines taste: crisp, clean, earthy, fruity, and vibrant."

f /liquiditybistro   🐦 @liquiditybistro   liquiditywines.com

The Farmers ❖ Boyd & Joan Collins
Poco A' Poco, Okanagan Falls

Boyd and Joan Collins have a small hobby farm that has become an exclusive grower for Rob Walker at Liquidity Bistro. As Boyd explains, their farm is located just a "hop, skip, and a jump from the Bistro," and he recalls his first visit for lunch, when he overheard the chef asking a local about finding local producers. He jumped in and introduced himself, and the two have been working together ever since.

Boyd explains, "The farm is named 'Poco A' Poco,' which means 'little by little' in Spanish. The projects of building the house, landscaping, and adding a small orchard, vineyard, and vegetable boxes were done little by little over ten years."

Boyd and his wife moved back to BC from Ontario in 2003, and didn't plan to get into farming at this level. But with "mentors all over the valley," Boyd explains that for each new planting on the farm, they had "someone new to teach us." He says, "People here are so supportive." They now have two acres filled with fruit trees, vegetables, and their famous blackberries. The variety is called Black Satin and chef Walker says they are "hands down the best blackberries I've ever had."

Besides growing for Liquidity Bistro, they have a few other regular customers, including a large following of devotees to Joan's amazing jams (she made 400 jars last year!). Your best bet to get your paws on a jar of the jam is to head over to the Bear Bean coffee shop in OK Falls, where they sell it.

The Winemaker ❖ Alison Moyes
Liquidity Wines, Okanagan Falls

Liquidity Wines offers a most extraordinary view of Okanagan Falls wine country. Perfectly angled to capture the rolling hills, vineyards, and Vaseaux Lake beyond, it is simply breathtaking. Winemaker Alison Moyes happily joined the team in 2015 and loves her new winery home base in Okanagan Falls. It is a region that has recently jumped into the big time, producing fantastic wines and offering wine lovers a destination region, with restaurants like Liquidity Bistro adding exponentially to the experience. Alison finds the local Okanagan Falls wine industry "so supportive" and speaks to the unique terroir saying, "The combination of soils and climate have proven to grow excellent Chardonnay and Pinot Noir—this region is becoming a world-class destination."

f /liquiditywines   🐦 @liquiditywines   liquiditywines.com

The Fixx Meatloaf Sandwich

LISA CHAM

THE ILLICHMANN FAMILY

GEHRINGER BROTHERS ESTATE WINERY

Are you looking for a comfort-food fix? This sandwich packs a wallop of flavour and home-cooked goodness, but with that special touch from a chef. Lisa Cham of the Fixx Café & Pasta Bar in Kelowna cooks to feed and please, and puts a good dose of love into all of her food. Make this for the family or friends and wait for the hugs.

Serves 6

Enjoy with 2014 Rosebud Rosé, Gehringer Brothers Estate Winery

Delicate splashes of strawberry, cranberry, rose petal, red currant and Granny Smith apple with a refreshingly dry finish.

Preheat the oven to 400°F (200°C). In a bowl, combine breadcrumbs, dry mustard, black pepper, garlic powder, basil, and oregano. Add ground meat and onion to the mixture and combine with hands.

In a separate bowl, whisk together eggs, Tabasco, Worcestershire, Dijon mustard, ketchup, and horseradish then add to the meat mixture and combine.

Place in a 9- × 5-inch (23 cm × 12 cm) loaf pan and bake for one hour.

Serve as a main or as part of a delicious sandwich like Lisa makes.

Sandwich assembly: Put together the meatloaf, sliced cheddar and Monterey cheese, mayonnaise, lettuce, and tomato on the focaccia buns. Lisa uses Bread on Wheels focaccia bread.

1½ cups (325 mL) fresh breadcrumbs, torn into chunks

1½ Tbsp (22 mL) dry mustard

1 tsp (5 mL) black pepper

1½ Tbsp (22 mL) garlic powder

1 Tbsp (15 mL) dry basil

1 Tbsp (15 mL) dry oregano

2½ pounds (1 kg) equal parts ground veal, beef, and pork (Illichmann's will blend for you)

1½ cups (325 mL) onion, finely diced

4 eggs

½ tsp (2.5 mL) Tabasco sauce

1½ tsp (7.5 mL) Worcestershire sauce

2 tsp (10 mL) Dijon mustard

¾ cup (175 ml) ketchup

1½ tsp (7.5 mL) horseradish

6 foccacia buns (if making sandwiches)

LISA CHAM

The Chef ❖ Lisa Cham
The Fixx Café & Pasta Bar, Kelowna

Lisa's lovely little bistro, the Fixx Café & Pasta Bar, quickly built and maintained a very loyal clientele since it opened. It is not only due to her good food—she is an amazing host and makes guests feel like they are dinner guests in her home. And it *is* her home—she is there all the time; it is the kind of neighbourhood bistro that becomes a habit.

Lisa operated Allegro Cafe in Vancouver before leaving it all for the sunshine and relocating to the Caribbean until 2004. "I stumbled onto Kelowna after I left Saint Vincent in 2004," Lisa explains. "I was visiting my family in Salmon Arm at the time and decided to make a trip to Kelowna to check it out. At the time, I was looking for my next venture, and after negotiations I bought the Fixx Cafe and moved to

Kelowna in January of 2005. I opened it for business on January 28. The rest is history."

Direct relationships are important to Lisa and to her cooking philosophy. "I love so many things about Kelowna as a chef. I love how I can receive a variety of fresh fish from Codfathers Seafood Market. Don at L&D Meats supplies me with fresh chicken and pork from the Lower Mainland; the family at Illichmann's supply me with the best fresh-ground meats for my bolognaise and meatloaf; and my friend Curtis has been running his local urban farm, Green City Acres, and supplies me with his amazing greens almost all year 'round. The lovely Alcock family that runs Sunshine Farms grows the best vegetables, which I receive on a weekly basis throughout the summer and fall, and Klemens from Bread on Wheels bakes and delivers my bread supply. All of these relationships make it fun and interesting to be a chef here in Kelowna."

🐦 @fixxcafe   thefixxcafe.com

The Butchers ❖ The Illichmann Family
Illichmann's Meats, Sausages and Gourmet Foods, Kelowna

An institution in Kelowna, Illichmann's Meats, Sausages and Gourmet Foods has been a beloved neighbourhood sausage maker and butcher since 1967. The fourth generation of Illichmanns continues the tradition, with son Tom, and his boys Jacob and Daniel, taking over from his parents, original owners Adolf and Theresia. Tom has expanded operations with catering, custom sausage making, and a bakery next door.

Daughter Judith Mercer (née Illichmann) shares the wonderful the family history: "We are originally from what is now the Czech Republic. My grandfather started a business like this one in 1931 as a master sausage maker and butcher. He had a meat shop and deli in Rotwasser, Czechoslovakia. After the war, he and his family ended up in Germany, where my father apprenticed as a sausage maker and butcher in Fulda, Hesse,

LEFT TO RIGHT: JUDITH MERCER (NÉE ILLICHMANN), ADOLF, SHARON, THOMAS, THERESIA, DANNY & JACOB ILLICHMANN

GORDON & WALTER GEHRINGER

West Germany. The family immigrated to Canada in the late 50s where my grandfather started again with a butcher shop and deli in Calgary. In 1967, my parents, wanting to start out on their own, moved to Kelowna and opened up a butcher shop and deli next to our present location. Back then it was the edge of town, and people asked my parents why they would open up a store 'way out there.' My parents built the present store in 1972.

My brother Thomas and his wife, Sharon, took over the business in the 90s. Thomas studied at Okanagan College's culinary program and trained in Europe. My parents are officially retired, but are still actively involved. Over the years everyone in the family has worked at the shop—Thomas, our younger brother Robert, and I grew up living (in the apartment) over the shop, and worked there after school and weekends." Seven grandchildren have also worked, or are currently working, at Illichmann's.

"Trends come and go, but quality and honest service is the benchmark of our family. The business has changed over the years in small ways, but the essential core of Illichmann's is always the same: a respect for the food we produce and a respect for the customers we produce it for. We love what we do. Otherwise one does not stay in business for four generations!"

f /Illichmann-Meats-Sausages-Gourmet-Foods-Ltd   illichmanns.com

The Winemaker ❖ Gordon & Walter Gehringer
Gehringer Brothers Estate Winery, Oliver

Gehringer Brothers Estate Winery is located just south of Oliver in the legendary grape-growing region coined the Golden Mile. Father Helmut Gehringer and his three sons, Walter, Gordon, and Karl, purchased their vineyard in 1981 and built the winery in 1985. Walter and Gordon both went to Germany to study wine and viticulture, returning with degrees and a great passion to make wine. Gehringer Brothers wine has become known as "King of the Platinum" by the judges at the Wine Press Northwest "Best of the Best" Platinum Wine Competition, for its consistent, double platinum and platinum wine awards. Gehringer Brothers has produced the most platinum medal-winning Rieslings, beating out many other renowned Riesling producers from north and south of the border.

The winery offers an impressive repertoire of 21 wines that are consistently produced at very reasonable prices. The Rosebud Rosé is lovingly named for Walter and Annemarie Gehringer's daughter, Liana, who passed away in May 2015. Annemarie explains, "Rosebud refers to her as being like a beautiful rose, still in its delicate bud phase, when she left us. The name is very fitting. Liana was 24, and had suffered with her illness for over ten years. She was a beautiful figure skater, pianist, singer, artist, and academic."

f /gehringer-brothers-estate-winery   🐦 @gb_wines   gehringerwines.ca

CLOCKWISE FROM TOP LEFT:

ROD'S ROOT VEGETABLE TORTE (P. 149),

EVELYNN'S ROASTED BRUSSELS SPROUT SALAD (P. 148),

ROBYN'S RED WINE-STEWED PLUM CRÊPES (P. 151), AND

BROCK'S 63 ACRES BRAISED BONE-IN BEEF SHORT RIBS

(P. 150)

RauDZ Sunday Night Supper

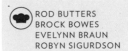

ROD BUTTERS
BROCK BOWES
EVELYNN BRAUN
ROBYN SIGURDSON

TONY CETINSKI

MIKE NIKOLAISEN

GRANT STANLEY

The team at RauDZ Regional Table and micro bar • bites in Kelowna has provided the recipes for you to create a stunning RauDZ-esque dinner party. It is served family style, preferably on a long table, with good wine (in this case we have paired the amazing Pinot Noir from 50th Parallel Estate Winery) and of course, friends and loved ones to enjoy it with. This menu, like all things created in the RauDZ kitchen, was created with love and with a dedication to the many farmers and artisans they work alongside. So, when you are shopping for this meal, please, follow our lead and buy local!

Menu

Roasted Brussels Sprout Salad, Pancetta with
Apple Vinaigrette & Grilled Kale

Root Vegetable Torte

63 Acres Braised Bone-In Beef Short Ribs

Red Wine-Stewed Plum Crêpes, Balsamic
Caramel Sauce, Chantilly Cream & Hazelnut Praline

Roasted Brussels Sprout Salad, Pancetta with Apple Vinaigrette & Grilled Kale

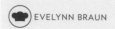 EVELYNN BRAUN

Finally, a solution to the age-old question: How do I make Brussels sprouts taste good? Evelynn has the answer and has created this amazing mélange of flavours that perfectly complements the essence of the Brussels sprout. The presentation is beautiful and you can make it ahead of time. Voila!

Serves 4–6

Preheat oven to 400°F (200°C). Clean Brussels sprouts, removing outer leaves (keep separated), and slice in half. Blanch Brussels sprouts in boiling water for 6 minutes and Brussels sprout leaves for 3 minutes; shock in an ice bath to stop the cooking process. Dry on a paper towel, then transfer to a baking sheet, drizzle with olive oil, and season with salt and pepper. Roast for 5–7 minutes, stirring occasionally. Once roasted, cool and set aside.

Toss apples in olive oil and apple juice and then roast in oven on baking sheet for 10–12 minutes.

On another baking sheet, lay pancetta in a single layer and bake until golden and crispy. Remove and place on paper towel to dry off excess fat.

Make vinaigrette. In a food processor, purée 2 roasted apples (reserving other 2 for salad) with mustard, honey, and vinegar. Slowly add oil to emulsify. Season with salt and pepper. Add pancetta.

Remove ribs from kale, toss with olive oil, and salt and pepper. Grill on BBQ until lightly charred.

To serve, toss roasted Brussels sprouts, remaining roasted apple slices, and Brussels sprouts leaves together in large bowl with desired amount of vinaigrette. Remaining vinaigrette can be refrigerated and kept for 7–10 days.

Top with grilled kale and extra pancetta. Enjoy!

3 lbs (1.4 kg) Brussels sprouts
extra virgin olive oil
salt and pepper
4 apples (Honeycrisp or Gala preferred), cored and sliced into ¼-inch (6-mm) wedges
1 cup + 2 Tbsp (280 mL) apple juice
6–8 slices mild pancetta
2 Tbsp (30 mL) Dijon mustard
2 Tbsp (30 mL) honey
1 cup + 2 Tbsp (280 mL) apple cider vinegar
2 cups (500 mL) grapeseed (or vegetable) oil
1 bunch kale

Root Vegetable Torte

This beautiful torte is a delicious work of art. The vibrant, colourful layers of the local, organic root vegetables provide a wonderful show of presentation, and the earthy, rich flavours highlighted by the herbs and goat cheese are a party on the palate. Do use a mandoline; buy one if you don't have one—these layers need to be sliced thinly and evenly for the best effect.

Serves 4–6

Pre-heat oven to 400°F (200°C). Spray an 8- × 8-inch (20 cm × 20 cm) casserole dish with non-stick spray or line entire dish with parchment paper. (If wanting to pre-slice, parchment paper will help remove the torte from dish.)

Layer one variety of vegetable at a time in dish. Between each layer, sprinkle garlic, shallots, Parmesan, cream, herbs, salt, and pepper. Continue to alternate vegetables until casserole dish is full. Try alternating different colours of vegetables for the greatest effect. Sprinkle goat cheese on top layer. Cover very loosely with tin foil or parchment paper. Casserole dish can be placed on a baking sheet in case liquid comes out while baking. Bake at 400°F (200°C) for approximately 50–60 minutes or until centre of casserole is fork-tender. Remove from oven and let stand. This can be served directly from the pan. Casserole can be cooked day before and chilled. The torte can then be removed from dish, sliced, and reheated. This recipe can be adapted without using cream or cheese. Substitute a sodium-free vegetable stock in place of cream.

3 cloves garlic, minced

3 large shallots, sliced thin

½ cup (125 mL) Parmesan cheese, shredded (or your choice of cheese)

1 cup (250 mL) heavy cream

¼ cup (60 mL) fresh herbs (your choice), chopped

*All vegetables to be peeled and sliced as thin as possible using mandoline or knife

2 large carrots

2 large beets, red and/or gold

1 medium rutabaga

2 medium white turnips

6 sunchokes (if available

1 small celery root

2 medium parsnips

2 russet potatoes

3 oz (90 g) mild goat cheese e.g., Happy Days Chèvre

sea salt

cracked black pepper

63 Acres Braised Bone-In Beef Short Ribs

 BROCK BOWES

A more flavourful, aromatic braising sauce I dare you to find! These tender short ribs luxuriate in the flavours of the sauce, infusing them with layers of goodness. Make sure to do the last step and make the sauce to serve at the table—with lots of bread-(we use our friend Monika the Baker's bread from Okanagan Grocery Artisan Breads Bakery, another favourite supplier at RauDZ).

Serves 4–6

The day before you make the short ribs, marinate them overnight with the onions, fennel, celery, carrots, garlic, cherries, red wine, stock, rosemary, thyme, bay leaves, and star anise.

The next day, preheat the oven to 375°F (190°C). Pull the short ribs out of marinade and pat dry with paper towel. Strain the remaining liquid out and keep separate from the vegetables. Season each short rib generously with salt. Coat the bottom of an ovenproof pot large enough to accommodate all the meat with olive oil, and put on high heat. Add the short ribs and brown very well, about 2–4 minutes per side (this may need to be done in two parts to avoid overcrowding the pot).

Set aside the browned short ribs and add the vegetables and tomato paste to the pot. Keeping the pot on high heat, sauté the vegetables and tomato paste until browned, stirring constantly to avoid burning.

Deglaze the pot using the wine and stock mixture. Add the short ribs back to the pot with the peppercorns and add more liquid to cover them if necessary. Cover with foil and put into the oven for about 2 ½ to 3 hours. Check periodically during the braising process and add more stock or water, if needed. Turn the ribs over halfway through the cooking time. Remove the foil for the last 20 minutes to let the meat brown and the sauce reduce. When finished, the meat should be soft and tender, but not falling apart; the bones should easily slide away from the meat. Gently pull out the ribs and reduce the liquid to a sauce consistency. Strain the sauce though a fine mesh strainer and check for seasoning. Assemble the short ribs onto a platter. Pour the finished sauce over the ribs or serve in a jug on the side, and finish the meat with a sprinkling of good sea salt. Enjoy!

4–8 (depending on size) 63 Acres bone-in beef short ribs

2 medium white onions, medium dice

1 large fennel bulb, medium dice

4 stalks celery, medium dice

4 large carrots, medium dice

1 bulb of garlic, peeled and smashed

2 cups (500 mL) cherries (fresh or frozen)

1 bottle (750 mL) Okanagan red wine (preferably Pinot Noir)

4 cups (1 L) beef or vegetable stock

4 stalks fresh rosemary

1 fistful fresh thyme

4 bay leaves

½ cup (125 mL) star anise pods

salt

1 cup (250 mL) extra virgin olive oil

1 cup (250 mL) tomato paste

sea salt

small handful of black peppercorns

Red Wine-Stewed Plum Crêpes, Balsamic Caramel Sauce, Chantilly Cream & Hazelnut Praline

ROBYN SIGURDSON

It is hard to describe just how amazing this dessert is. It is a symphony of flavours. Each is distinct and perfect on its own, but together they reach a crescendo. Be prepared to break out into song.

Serves 4–6

In a blender, combine all ingredients and mix on medium speed for 2 minutes until well combined

Place in fridge for 1 hour.

Slightly oil a Teflon non-stick pan, place on medium heat.

Once pan is hot, take your pan to your bowl of batter. Pour a small ladle worth into the middle of the pan and quickly swirl around until pan is covered. Try to get crêpes as thin as possible. Return to heat and cook until bubbles start to form in the middle. You should have a beautiful golden-brown crêpe.

Cool on a baking sheet, then wrap in plastic or store in an airtight container.

In a medium saucepan, combine plums, brown sugar, and cinnamon cook for 2 minutes, then add 1 cup (250 mL) red wine and vanilla bean, and cook out until plums start to soften, approximately 10 minutes. Whisk together the cornstarch and red wine and then add to plums. Cook out for 5 minutes; adjust if you want your plums a little sweeter. Pour into a dish and cool immediately for use later or serve warm.

Caramel: In a medium pot with a lid, add sugar to the water. Keep pot at medium heat, checking occasionally; do not stir. Once it turns caramel colour, remove from heat and pour in whipping cream and whisk quickly. Be careful—sugar will be very hot. Once fully incorporated, add balsamic vinegar and cool. Place in an airtight container. Serve warm.

Cream: In a mixer with the whisk attachment, whip cream until medium peaks form.

Add sugar and vanilla and whip until stiff.

Praline: Place roasted hazelnuts on a parchment-covered baking tray.

In a small pot, add sugar and water, then cover.

Cook until caramel colour forms. Pour over hazelnuts. Be careful—it will be extremely hot.

Cool at room temperature until hard. Then remove from parchment, place in your food processor for a couple seconds or use a knife and chop it up to desired consistency. Store in an airtight container at room temperature.

To serve, lay your beautiful crêpes out on a plate. Serve alongside warmed stewed plums, balsamic caramel, Chantilly cream, and a little bowl of hazelnut praline. Enjoy!

Crêpes

1½ cups (375 mL) 2% milk

3 eggs

1¼ cups (310 mL) flour

2 tsp (10 mL) sugar

1 tsp (5 mL) vanilla extract

Red wine-stewed plums

10–12 medium Okanagan plums (you can use frozen), halved and pitted

½ cup (125 mL) brown sugar

½ tsp (2.5 mL) ground cinnamon

1 cup (250 mL) red wine (suggested: 50th Parallel Pinot Noir) +6 Tbsp (90 mL)

½ vanilla bean, scraped

1 tsp (5 mL) cornstarch

Balsamic caramel

1 cup (250 mL) white sugar

½ cup (125 mL) water

¾ cup (175 mL) whipping cream

2 Tbsp (30 mL) balsamic vinegar

Chantilly cream

2 cups (500 mL) whipping cream

¼ cup (60 mL) icing sugar, sifted

1 tsp (5 mL) vanilla extract

Hazelnut praline

1 cup (250 mL) white sugar

½ cup (125 mL) water

¼ cup (60 mL) hazelnuts (or whatever nuts you choose), roasted and peeled

LEFT TO RIGHT: GRANT STANLEY, ROBYN SIGURDSON, BROCK BOWES, ROD BUTTERS, EVELYNN BRAUN

The Chef ✤ Rod Butters
RauDZ Creative Concepts, Kelowna

Superstar local chef Rod Butters and his partner Audrey Surrao, together as RauDZ Creative Concepts, have built three legendary Okanagan restaurants. The first Okanagan endeavour was launched as Fresco, a restaurant that sent a supersonic shock through the regional culinary landscape, transforming local restaurant standards forever. Fresco won multiple awards, so when the announcement came that they were reopening under a new name and new brand in 2009, fans and media were gobsmacked. How could they compete with the legend? Well, they did, and they surpassed the Fresco brand with RauDZ Regional Table, which was followed in 2013 by micro bar • bites, a baby sister located up the street that focuses on drinks and small dishes.

The RauDZ brand was built on, and lives and breathes, the concept of farm-to-table and supporting local farmers and artisans. The walls in RauDZ are testament to this—they are lined with photographs of the farmers, fishmongers, and winemakers that supply them. Rod explains, "Community: a simple word that means so much. Whether you are a chef, a cheese maker, a fishmonger, raising free-range chickens, making world-class wines, or an inspired home cook, we are all part of the community of food. We share a love and a passion for food; this is what holds our community together."

This philosophy goes way back. Rod Butters was the first chef de cuisine to open the über-famous Relais & Châteaux restaurant, The Pointe at the Wickaninnish Inn in Tofino. It was there that he began dialing up local farmers and fisherman. This was an absolutely new concept in a time when importing ingredients was the norm.

In 2015, Rod decided to step back from the kitchen and hired a new chief for his team: Brock Bowes, a chef with an impressive resume, and whose ethics were instilled by Rod's friend and esteemed colleague chef Bernard Casavant. Brock as executive chef working with chef Evelynn Takoff and chef Robyn Sigurdson is a dream team of culinary talent, and they are carrying on Rod's legacy with great passion. And in Rod's words, "When you cook with passion, you feed the soul."

The Chef ❖ Brock Bowes
RauDZ Creative Concepts, Kelowna

Brock Bowes graduated from the Vancouver Island University Culinary Arts program and went on to work under (now local) esteemed chef Bernard Casavant at the Fairmont Chateau Whistler. After travelling in Europe, Brock returned to the valley in 2013 took over the kitchen at Burrowing Owl's Sonora Room Restaurant for a year. As leader of the new team at RauDZ, Brock explains, "Our success comes from being a team in which each member has each other's back from all points of the kitchen. We collaborate on all parts of our menus and day-to-day operations." On working in the Okanagan, he says, "My inspiration comes from where we live and all the amazing products from our farms, wineries, fish mongers, meat producers—where else in Canada would you want to live if you chef?"

In 2015, chef Bowes won the Chopped Canada competition. He also represented RauDZ Creative Concepts and the Okanagan Valley in the 2016 Canadian Culinary Championships Gold Medal Plates in Victoria.

The Chef ❖ Evelynn Braun
RauDZ Creative Concepts, Kelowna

Evelynn Braun (née Takoff) is one half of one of the Okanagan's culinary power couples. Her husband is chef Chris Braun at micro bar • bites, and together they represent a great passion for cooking and respect for the farmer.

On RauDZ, Evelynn adds, "Our restaurant philosophy is local, fresh, comfortable—it speaks for itself as to why we love cooking in the Okanagan."

Both Evelynn and Chris were raised on farms, with hard work and sustainability practice ingrained in them from a young age. Now with their own little guy, baby Sebastian, the couple will pass on their philosophies to the next generation. She says, "I was born and raised in Kelowna. And now I'm starting my own family here. I couldn't imagine raising him anywhere else than the Okanagan. We love it here! My creativity stems from what is around us—like what produce and livestock is available based on the seasons. I love having a close relationship with our suppliers and being able to feed off of their enthusiasm for their products."

Not only a local star, Evelynn also competed on Food Network's *Top Chef Canada* television series in 2014!

The Chef ❖ Robyn Sigurdson
RauDZ Creative Concepts, Kelowna

Now the chef de cuisine at RauDZ, Robyn has worked with some of the Okanagan's finest chefs. Her resume and talent led her to win the Okanagan Chef's Association Farm to Fork competition in 2010, which sent her to Italy to work on an *agriturismo* farm for three months.

Born and raised in the Okanagan, Robyn graduated from the Okanagan College Culinary Program. She says, "The Okanagan is truly a chef's playground. We have some of the best farmers and chefs, and the finest products you will find across Canada, but it's the people and the camaraderie that make the Okanagan the best place to cook."

A strong believer in the farm-to-table cooking philosophy, she shares, "When you have the opportunity to walk the property of a farmer's land, it changes your perspective of those carrots, beets, and apricots that come in the back door. It humbles you as a cook to have the opportunity to be able to create something beautiful on the plate. The relationship between restaurants and their suppliers is so important for the continued growth of the farm-to-plate way of cooking. That relationship allows the kitchen to receive amazing local products that we take pride in putting on a plate; it also allows the supplier to have their business prosper and continue a legacy of farming that has continued for decades."

RauDZ Regional Table: **f** /raudz /microkelowna 🐦 @raudz @raudzbar raudz.com

micro bar • bites: **f** /microkelowna 🐦 @MicroKelowna microkelowna.com

TONY CETINSKI

produce food. I prefer to think of my fields as a pantry, not a warzone."

Thankfully, the community is slowly beginning to change its consumer habits by sourcing more local products. Tony says, "I think that people are looking for more value in their food choices. I like to say that when we started people were often looking for the cheapest food they could find, but are now looking for the best food they can afford. Large retailers certainly have their place, but people are more aware of the difference fresh makes. I would like to see more awareness of the importance of eating seasonally appropriate food—for example, fresh peaches should not be expected in Kelowna in January. Our relationship with local chefs is critical to our farm's future. They truly value our product and really understand what we do."

250-801-2843

The Farmers ❖ Tony & Nancy Cetinski
Suncatcher Farm, Kelowna

"The greatest fine art of the future will be the making of a comfortable living from a small piece of land."
—Abraham Lincoln

The Cetinskis have been one of the RauDZ team's main suppliers for years. The Kelowna-based farm operation has a really interesting history. Tony explains, "We bought our farm in 2001 with rose-coloured glasses firmly in place. I had never farmed a day in my life, but had always thought it would be a great lifestyle. Our farm is part of the oldest farmstead in Kelowna. The original owner was Eli Lequime; he bought a 160-acre parcel in 1885. To put that into context, our copy of the original deed was signed on behalf of Queen Victoria. He had three sons, Bernard, Lawrence, and Leon.

"We grow Canada-certified organic mixed vegetables on about 5 acres. It is light work—when it's light, I work. Organic is just a simpler, more natural way to

The Rancher ❖ Mike Nikolaisen
Miane Creek Livestock for 63 Acres Beef, Armstrong

63 Acres is a local brand of premium Angus cross beef raised on selected partner farms in the Armstrong area of the Okanagan. Mike Nikolaisen's Miane Creek Livestock is the main partner farm that helps source cattle for the brand. Mike has been a cattle rancher his whole life and takes pride in the beef he produces. The beef is free-range, grass-fed, and grain-finished, without any added hormones or steroids (growth promotants).

Chris Les from 63 Acres explains their concept: "Originally we had thought of purchasing beef from BC producers scattered all over the province, including setting up our own farm in the Fraser Valley where we could bring potential customers for tours. We started working with our marketing people on a new potential brand name for the line, and one of the ones they came up with is 63 Acres. '63' refers to the average number of head in a typical BC herd of cattle (per some government statistics they'd uncovered). At the same time (summer 2014), we were looking at property in

MIKE NIKOLAISEN

ANNABEL & GRANT STANLEY

the Fraser Valley to set up a 'tour-able' working farm. We'd focused in on one particular property that was 85 acres in size, in two parcels. The plan was to sell one of the parcels, which was 22 acres, leaving—you guessed it—63 acres for our showcase farm. It seemed the writing was on the wall, so we moved forward with the brand while we continued to do due diligence on the farm. In the end, the farm deal didn't work out, but we've kept the brand."

63acresbeef.com

The Winemaker ❖ Grant Stanley
50th Parallel Estate Winery, Lake Country

This is a rockstar winery team (seriously, and they all look like rockstars). As friendly and passionate about their winery as they are glamourous, Sheri-Lee Turner-Krouzel, Curtis Krouzel, and their star winemaker, Grant Stanley, are building a colossal new winery in Lake Country. The winemaking facility and tasting room are modern and meticulously planned, but the plans for the restaurant, accommodations, and event facilities will take the 50th over the top.

Grant Stanley is known for his Pinot Noir creations and his 50th Parallel versions will not disappoint. Grant is a dual citizen of Canada and New Zealand, and spent many years in the vineyards of kiwiland where he "became a willing and humble slave to the high priests of Pinot Noir in Martinborough." Grant was attracted to the Okanagan's potential to make great Pinot Noir and signed up with Quails' Gate Family Estate Winery, where he would remain for 10 years before joining 50th Parallel. He and his wife, Annabel, who operates her own vineyard from which she harvests both grapes and grapevines that she skill-fully trains into gorgeous sculptures, live the best of the Okanagan lifestyle with their son, Francis.

f 50thParallelEstate   🐦 @50thparallelwin   50thparallel.com

DESERTS

Sandrine's Lavender Crème Brûlée

SANDRINE MARTIN-RAFFAULT

ANDREA MCFADDEN

JEFF MARTIN

Could a dessert sound more delightful than this? Sandrine Martin-Raffault, the Okanagan's French superstar pastry chef, created it—everything she makes is *magnifique*. We are so lucky to have her bakery, Sandrine French Pastry & Chocolate, here in Kelowna!

Makes 6 large shallow ramekins

Enjoy with La Frenz Winery LV Liqueur Muscat

Alluring aromatics of rose petals and steeped Earl Grey tea draw you in. On the palate you will experience beautiful flavours of caramelized brown sugar, cinnamon and the nectar-like notes unique to the Muscat grape varietal.

Bring whipping cream and milk to a boil with the vanilla pod. Remove from heat and stir in the lavender flowers, and infuse for 10 to 15 minutes.

In the meantime, separate the eggs, weigh the sugar, and prepare a water bath (also know as a *bain-marie*) by adding medium-hot (not boiling) water to a baking dish and filling it until water is halfway up the sides of the ramekins. Strain the cream/milk mixture and let cool down.

When the mixture is warm, mix the eggs with the sugar and pour the cream on the eggs while stirring. Strain the mixture. Pour in the ramekins.

Bake in a water bath for 20 to 40 minutes at 275°F (135°C), until the crème in the middle of the ramekin is set. Remove the ramekins from the water bath.

Keep in the fridge overnight.

Before serving, sprinkle a thin layer of granulated sugar. Caramelize the sugar with a torch or in the oven on broil. Garnish crème brûlée with lavender. Enjoy as soon as the caramelized sugar is firm and cool. Raise your spoons and crack!

*When choosing the ramekins, it is best to use large shallow containers.

1 cup (250 mL) whipping cream
1 cup (250 mL) milk
½ vanilla pod (optional)
½ tsp (2.5 mL) lavender flowers from Okanagan Lavender Farm
9 egg yolks
½ cup (125 mL) sugar

LEFT TO RIGHT: ANDREA MCFADDEN & SANDRINE MARTIN-RAFFAULT

The Pastry Chef ❖ Sandrine Martin-Raffault
Sandrine French Pastry & Chocolate, Kelowna

Sandrine Martin-Raffault was born and raised in the Beaujolais region of France, and her family's history in the baking and pastry industry goes back four generations. She trained at her cousin's pastry and chocolate shop and attended culinary schools in Paris to hone her craft.

In 2004, Sandrine, her husband, Pierre-Jean, and their two children moved to the Okanagan. Their first shop, La Boulangerie Gourmet Café Ltd., offered locals a taste of France with breads, pastries, and savoury items. In 2010, they decided to focus on what Sandrine loved best and opened Sandrine French Pastry and Chocolate, a smaller shop specializing cakes, macarons, and chocolates. Walking through the front doors of Sandrine's, the display of handcrafted chocolates, multicoloured macarons, cakes, and other French delights will make your inner Parisian swoon. The pretty little cakes are as delicious as they are perfect looking, and will turn any occasion into a celebration. From the gourmet capital of the world, Sandrine brings the taste of France to the Okanagan. She also offers gourmet savouries—including delicious tourtière, quiche, pâté, and duck confit—for her happy customers to take home.

Sandrine offers pastry classes and hands-on workshops, where small groups of participants learn how to bake French cakes and desserts from scratch in Sandrine's professional kitchen.

Sandrine explains her passion: "Food is a crucial part of French life. In order to keep this strong relationship with food, while having busy lives, the French have developed a way of cooking that is simple, efficient, and easy to integrate into their lifestyle. In this spirit, we teach recipes that people can find time to bake at home and don't require specific skills or equipment. We want to encourage people to bake at home, have fun doing it, and enjoy the food they proudly baked. It is so nice to be able to introduce participants to French baking, and share recipes and stories. The main reward is to see them so proud of their baking successes. The lavender crème brûlée is one of my favourite recipes as it is simple and fast to bake, but mainly because lavender is, to me, the perfect image of the Okanagan that reminds me of France."

f sandrinefrenchpastryandchocolate   🐦 @sandrinepastry   sandrinepastry.com

The Lavender Farmer ❖ Andrea McFadden
Okanagan Lavender & Herb Farm, Kelowna

Owner Andrea McFadden and her husband, David, have created a beautiful oasis on their southeast Kelowna lake-view property. Rows of lavender run down the property interspersed with herb plants, making this farm an amazing sensory experience. Lavender is believed to aid a multitude of problems, including stress, anxiety, headaches, insomnia, depression, colds, upset stomach, and nervousness. Its intoxicating scent can be distilled into an essential oil and used as perfume, or used medicinally when inhaled to induce relaxation, sleep, and ease stress. As a culinary herb, the scent and taste transform the most ordinary dish into something extraordinary. Because of its unique flavour, the addition of lavender adds a certain mystique, and visually, it's just so darn pretty.

The gift shop on the farm is loaded with aromatic delights. A distiller as well, Andrea makes several oils from her flowers and herbs. She offers all-natural skincare products to soothe a range of issues. She even has created a line of perfumes.

Andrea also gives a lot back to the community, generously hosting charity events as well as offering workshops. She loves to host workshops for children and introduce them to exciting new flavours and "teach them where food comes from." As the daughter of pioneer winery owner Dick Stewart of Quails' Gate Estate Winery, Andrea has farming in her genes. She says, "Our Irish grandfather arrived in the Okanagan in 1908. He paved the way for his descendants to embrace agriculture as a way of life, first working for David Gellatly at the historic Gellatly Nut Farm on the west side and then starting Stewart Brothers Nursery in Kelowna in 1911. Formerly an apple orchard, the farm now grows over 60 varieties of lavender and also has a u-pick bed to experience the *joie de vivre* of harvesting this soothing plant."

f /okanagan.lavender 🐦 @kelownalavender okanaganlavender.com

The Winemaker ❖ Jeff Martin
La Frenz Winery, Penticton

Australian-born Jeff Martin's passion for sustainable vineyard practices is inspiring. Jeff became involved in the wine industry at the age of 18, when renowned Australian producer McWilliams employed him as a trainee winemaker at its half-million-case Beelbangera facility. Years later, in 1989, Jeff became the chief red winemaker for the McWilliams group, with his wines winning major awards at Australian wine shows.

NIVA & JEFF MARTIN

Following a sabbatical in Napa, he and his wife, Niva, stopped over to see the Okanagan Valley and fell in love—and moved here in 1994. Jeff has built an almost self-sustainable ecosystem with his Naramata properties using Mother Nature as his vineyard manager. He explains, "It's about creating diversity in our vineyard environment, the opposite to modern farming monocultures where specializing in single crops and animals has created an overdependence on fossil fuels and a depletion of our resources. Farmers compensate by adding fertilizers and nutrients when nature and natural processes do a much better job of it."

f /lafrenzwinery 🐦 @lafrenzwinery lafrenzwinery.com

The Bench Raspberry Almond Tarts

STEWART GLYNES

JAMES YOUNG

RON TAYLOR

These pretty little tarts by Stewart Glynes of the Bench Market in Penticton can be as casual or as elegant as the event you choose to serve them at. The beautiful ruby red raspberries are like little jewels that can be deliciously crowned with some vanilla ice cream or a raspberry sauce.

Makes about 12 4-inch (10 cm) tarts

Enjoy with Sleeping Giant Raspberry Fruit Wine

Bursting with the rich flavour of fresh raspberries, this is a nice sipping wine that also lends itself beautifully to wine spritzers and fruit martinis. To pair with Stewart's dish, make a pretty pink spritzer with your favorite Okanagan dry white wine.

Make the almond filling. In your Kitchen Aid mixer, cream butter and sugar until smooth (approximately 7 minutes on medium-high speed). Add almond and eggs, one at a time, until incorporated. Add flour and mix on low until just combined. Set aside.

Make the pastry. Mix together flour, butter, and salt in bowl with hands until it is a fine sand-like texture. Add cold water a little at a time, until dough comes together but is not sticky. Form into flat dish shape and chill for 1 hour.

Preheat oven to 350°F (180°C). Place dough on floured surface and roll out to ¾-inch (2-cm) thickness. Cut with molds slightly larger than tart shells and fold into floured tart sheets and shape. For a 4-inch (10-cm) tart, add 5 or 6 raspberries to bottom of shell. Add enough almond cream to come even with top of tart. Press another 5 or 6 raspberries into top of almond cream in whatever design you like. Bake for approximately 15–20 minutes or until top is lightly brown around edge.

Best served warm but can be stored in an airtight container in the fridge for up to one week. Sprinkle with icing sugar before serving and a mint leaf if you wish.

Almond filling

1 cup (250 mL) butter
1 cup (250 mL) white sugar
1 cup (250 mL) almonds, ground
4 eggs
½ cup (125 mL) all-purpose flour

Pastry

2 cups (500 mL) all-purpose flour
⅔ cup (150 mL) cold unsalted butter
pinch of salt
3–5 Tbsp (45–75 mL) cold water
2 cups (500 mL) fresh raspberries

Serving

icing sugar, to finish
mint leaf, for garnish

LEFT TO RIGHT: JAMES YOUNG & STEWART GLYNES

from, what variety it is, and who grew it. One of our main farmers, who provides an assortment of fruit and vegetables from February to December, also takes all our fruit and vegetable trimmings, egg shells, coffee grounds etc., and composts it to fertilize his soil to provide new crops next year, to sell back to us. The compost enriches the produce he provides us, as well as lessening our environmental footprint, which is important to us. Our local support extends from our kitchen to the many Okanagan artisan retail products on our shelves."

Stewart was born to be a chef; his enthusiasm and passion for his craft is clear in his description of what attracted him to life in the kitchen: "The environment of a professional kitchen and the lifestyle was extremely intoxicating to me. The energy that I got from the sound of pans and dishes, oven doors opening and closing, loud music, voices of staff in constant communication with one another, and laughter of the guests having a great time was amazing!"

f /TheBenchMarket 🐦 @benchchef4 thebenchmarket.com

The Chef ❖ Stewart Glynes
The Bench Market, Penticton

Stewart and Heather Glynes moved to the Okanagan from the West Coast to raise their growing family. Now with three little ones, a successful catering business, and a neighbourhood restaurant to run, the two are living their dream. Community and sustainable business practices are important to the duo, and they are very active in fundraising and supporting community events. It is no surprise they were awarded the Penticton & Wine Country Chamber of Commerce 2015 Business Excellence Award for Sustainability.

"It is important to support those who support you," says Stewart. "We enjoy knowing people and what they do, why they do what they do, and the story of where their food comes from. The closer you are with your suppliers, the easier it is to create amazing, fresh, and tasty food. It also gives us the ability to tell customers the story of where a certain fruit or vegetable came

The Farmer ❖ James Young
Kitchen Garden Gourmet, Naramata

James and his wife, Julie, have created an extraordinary "kitchen garden" in the village of Naramata. They have transformed the property into a haven, growing a wide array of vegetables and fruits—including figs!

James is a registered nurse (RN), but has always kept his green thumb in the soil: "I grew up in Penticton after immigrating from England in 1962. My parents bought a 12-acre orchard on the Naramata Bench in 1972 that we turned into a mixed farm. We had a very large productive vegetable garden, 200–300 chickens, 30–70 sheep, pigs, and both beef cows and a dairy cow." The family returned to the UK in 1979, but the farm life drew him back to Naramata. He says, "In 2003 I moved to Naramata onto an 0.39-acre property. I took out 60 tons of tree stumps and over the next 12 years, developed the gardens into a boutique micro farm. I have a microclimate in the Naramata Creek valley, which gives me a cooler summer temperature in half the garden. 0.20 acres are used for production with most crops in raised bed and the strawberries in hanging baskets and elevated growing troughs."

A strong believer in community access to local produce and products, he continues: "My wife and I started the Naramata Community Farmers' Market in 2005 as there was no formal place to buy local produce in Naramata at that time. Two years ago I switched completely to direct sale to restaurants for my produce. My main crops now are strawberries, blackberries, raspberries, kales, basil, red and white table grapes, and garlic with fresh figs as of this year— the figs are just fun to grow and surprise chefs with as my trees start to produce a marketable crop. It gives me great pleasure to see the looks of amazement on people's faces as they discover my garden and what I can grow in such a small space."

RON TAYLOR

kitchengardengourmet.blogspot.ca

The Winemaker ❖ Ron Taylor
Sleeping Giant Fruit Winery

Summerland Sweets, Okanagan jam and syrup makers, owns Sleeping Giant Fruit Winery. The proprietor, Mr. F.E. (Ted) Atkinson, founded Summerland Sweets in 1962, and since then it has been a destination for visitors and locals who love sweets. Atkinson's dedication to preserving local fruits has won him longevity in this dying business. The Okanagan was filled with canneries and fruit-processing plants from the late 1800s up to the 1960s, when they began to disappear due to big corporate buyouts. A lesson in sustainability, Summerland Sweets not only creates jams, syrups, and brittles—they also utilize our local bounty in their fruit wines.

"He was also a very active member of the local Rotary Club and decided to make a fruit jelly candy to raise funds for the club. Working out of a pickers' cabin on his cherry orchard, he produced candy for the club for a couple of years before he turned to commercial production. What began as a fundraising effort grew into a retirement project and blossomed into Summerland Sweets Ltd.!"

Fruit winemaker Ron Taylor has a degree in microbiology from the University of British Columbia. No stranger to the wine industry, Ron spent 22 years at Andres Wines before he left in 1992 to consult for small wineries in the province. His expertise in turning grapes to wine took Sleeping Giant fruit wines to the next level.

f /sleepinggiantfruitwinery   🐦 @sleepinggiantbc   sleepinggiantfruitwinery.ca

Pepper Strawberry & Cream Pavlova
with Balsamic Vinegar

 ANNINA HOFFMEISTER

 ALOIS THURN

 JENNIFER TURTON-MOLGAT

This dessert is beautiful and elegant. The individual servings begin with a crunch and end with a surprising, creamy middle. The balsamic vinegar on the plate adds a lovely zip, and topping the dish with fresh flowers, like Annina did, will make you a star at your dinner party.

Makes 4–6

Enjoy with 2014 Distraction Frizzante, The View Winery
Aromas of strawberries, cranberry, and pomegranate bubble out of the glass. On the palate, summer's red berry fruit fills your mouth, followed by a lingering honey finish.

To make pavlova: Beat egg whites, sugar, and white vinegar in a mixer until hard peaks form. Add and carefully fold in the sugar, cornstarch, and lemon juice. When just combined, load into a piping bag, and with a No. 12 piping tip draw circles on a baking sheet and make little nests (or use a spoon.) Bake at 212°F (100°C) for about one hour. Turn oven off and let sit for 2 more hours. Can be made in advance and kept in airtight container at room temperature.

In a saucepan, slowly heat up milk, sugar and vanilla bean with scraped seeds.

Slightly whisk 4 egg yolks up in a bowl. Add milk mixture a little at time to temper. Pour back into saucepan and carefully boil until thickened. Pour through strainer and cover tightly with wrap. Place in fridge to cool.

Carefully wash strawberries and cut into quarters. Place in bowl. Add 2 oz of Grand Marnier and some freshly ground pepper. Let soak for about 2 hours.

Vanilla cream: Whip heavy cream until soft peaks form. Fold in Vanilla Cream and 2 oz of Grand Marnier. Place cream mixture on top of Pavlovas, top with strawberries, and garnish with icing-sugar-sprinkled fresh lemon balm and small dots of aged balsamic vinegar from Okanagan Vinegar Brewery to your liking.

Pavlova

4 egg whites, room
   temperature
(save 4 egg yolks for
   vanilla cream below)
¾ cup (190 mL) sugar
½ tsp (2.5 mL) white vinegar

Add and carefully fold in:

⅓ cup (75 mL) sugar
1 Tbsp (30 mL) corn
   starch, sifted
Juice from one lemon

Vanilla cream

Slowly heat up:
1¾ cups (400 mL) milk
¼ cup (60 mL) sugar
Seeds of ½ vanilla
   bean and bean
4 egg yolks
strawberries
2 oz Grand Marnier
1 tsp (5 mL) freshly ground
   black pepper
1 cup (250 mL) heavy
   cream (36%)
Fresh lemon balm, for garnish
Okanagan Vinegar Brewing
   aged balsamic vinegar

LEFT TO RIGHT: ANNINA AND JÖRG HOFFMEISTER

The Chef ❖ Annina Hoffmeister
doLci sociaLhouse, Osoyoos

Formerly known as Dolci Deli & Catering, proprietors Annina and Jörg Hoffmeister originally moved to Canada in 1997 to pursue their dream of owning a bakery/restaurant—and they succeeded. Both received their degrees in Europe, she in Switzerland and he, in Germany, and together they brought us their creative talents and passions and operated their very successful business for nine years. Sadly, Jörg passed away in 2013, leaving the community broken-hearted. He was a wonderful spirit, always ready with a saucy joke and a smile with a twinkle in his eye. That twinkle lives on through Annina and their daughter Jennifer.

Annina grew up in a picturesque, small ski village romantically located in the Swiss Alps. It was there that she fell in love with the art of pastry making. She

also loves the coziness of a small town and tight community, both of which she has found in Osoyoos. After Jörg's passing, she decided to start a new chapter in her life and recreated the deli business into more of a local hub, a 'socialhaus,' like in Europe, where community meets. The front room at doLci sociaLhouse is cozy and hip and the back garden patio remains a secret hideaway, where guests can have a party or enjoy an intimate meal for two. As was the focus at the deli, the menu focuses on fresh local produce and a locally sourced wine list featuring many of their award-winning neighbours. Calling the menu "local food with world inspired twists," Annina carries on Jörg's legacy of house made charcuterie serving favorites like the Osoyoos Applewood smoked bacon, salami and Annnina's favorite, Bundnerfleisch (a tasty air-dried Swiss meat).

f /dolci-socialhaus   🐦 @ doLcisociaLhaus   dolcideli.com

The Vinegar Maker ❖ Alois Thurn
Okanagan Vinegar Brewery, Summerland

Alois Thurn moved to Canada in 1982 from Marmagen, Germany, an agricultural region near Cologne. With a rich history in family farming—traceable back to 1117 (also the name of his winery)– the creation of food runs deep in his blood.

Alois has always worked in the food industry; he is a trained sausage maker and has consulted on various industry levels. His excellent palate and industrious nature lead him into the exciting world of vinegar brewing. Because the creation of true vinegars, like his rich and delicious balsamico, need years to age, just like a fine wine, Thurn has had time to follow other projects like buying and planting a vineyard. In 2015, he opened his winery, Bodega 1117.

Besides wine, Thurn's product line now includes five categories: wine vinegars, fruit vinegars, balsamic vinegars, wine jellies and condiments. His wine vinegars include a sherry wine, Riesling white wine and Champagne vinegar, and the fruit vinegars are black

ALOIS THURN

JENNIFER TURTON-MOLGAT

cherry, raspberry and apple. The intense and gorgeous Solera 2000 is a rich Pinot Noir balsamico that has been aged in the barrique style (Bordeaux barrels) for six years.

250-809-2077

Turton had the foresight to replant part of his orchard with cider apples (and then, later on, grapevines). Both ventures proved extremely successful with both Ward's Hard Cider and The View Winery becoming two local favorites.

f /the-view-winery   @theviewwinery   theviewwinery.com

The Winemaker ❖ Jennifer Turton-Molgat
The View Winery, Kelowna

Stylish "Head Diva" at The View Winery, Jennifer Turton-Molgat has a family history in local tree fruit farming going back five generations. The View's tasting room, located on Ward Road in Kelowna, is actually the original packinghouse built by Great-Granddad Ward in 1922. Jen says, "These rich and fruitful lands have been nurtured by the Wards/Turtons since the initial plantings by my great-grandfather George Ward in the early 1920s." Jennifer's father Chris

Poplar Grove Double Cream Camembert Cheesecake with Rhubarb Compote

JENNA PILLON

GITTA PEDERSEN

ROB SUMMERS

You may think you have had cheesecake, but cheesecake made with Poplar Grove cheese is a revelation! After the photoshoot, I had the pleasure of ravaging this cake with Jenna, Gitta and April Goldade—along with some lovely wine, of course.

Makes 8–10 portions

Enjoy with Late Harvest Pinot Blanc, Hester Creek Winery

This honeyed late harvest offers flavours of juicy orchard fruits,
like peaches and nectarines, balanced with refreshing acidity.

Preheat oven to 375°F (190°C). Cream butter, sugars, cinnamon, and cloves together. Add flour, baking soda, and salt to creamed mixture. Stir together until combined and then cool in fridge for 30 minutes. Roll out on floured surface to ⅛-inch (3-mm) thick, bake for 7–10 minutes, and then buzz in a food processor. Spread out evenly the desired amount on the bottom of 9-inch (23 cm) glass pie plate.

Base: Preheat oven to 325°F (160°C). In a food processor, add cream cheese, Camembert, and sugar. Process until very smooth. Add eggs, one at a time, then vanilla, and salt. Make sure to scrape down the sides. Add the sour cream and blend; add the whipping cream and process until combined. Pour on top of graham cracker base. Depending on the pan you are using and how thick the filling is will determine how long it will take to bake. You don't want any colour, but the centre shouldn't move when the dish is shaken. Bake for roughly 30–45 minutes.

Chef's tip: Put a pot of water in the stove next to the pie to create moisture to help the filling from cracking.

Once set, turn off the oven and leave the door open a crack for 45 minutes then remove to a rack to cool for 2 hours. Once cooled, move into the fridge for at least 8 hours to set properly.

Compote: Pick the reddest rhubarb you can find for the best colour and flavour. Combine all of ingredients in a pot. Cook on low-to-medium heat until soft. Adjust sugar to taste and pour over cake to serve.

Graham cracker base

¾ cup (190 mL) soft butter +
  2 Tbsp (30 mL)
½ cup (125 mL) brown sugar
¼ cup (60 mL) icing sugar
1 tsp (5 mL) ground cinnamon
¼ tsp (1 mL) cloves
1½ cups (325 mL) flour
½ tsp (2.5 mL) baking soda
¼ tsp (1 mL) salt

Cheesecake base

2⅓ cup (575 mL) cream cheese
  (room temperature)
1½ cups (2 wheels) Poplar Grove
  Double Cream Camembert
  (room temperature)
1⅓ cup (325 mL)
  granulated sugar
4 large eggs
1 tsp (5 mL) vanilla
½ tsp (2.5 mL) salt
⅔ cup (150 mL) sour cream
⅔ cup (150 mL) whipping
  cream

Rhubarb compote

6 cups (2.2 lbs) rhubarb,
  chopped
3 Tbsp (45mL) white
  balsamic vinegar
3 Tbsp (45mL) granulated
  sugar

LEFT TO RIGHT: JENNA PILLON & GITTA PEDERSEN

The Chef ✤ Jenna Pillon
Terrafina Restaurant at Hester Creek, Oliver

Terrafina means "from the earth" and you will be swept away by the romantic setting of this eatery located on Oliver's "Golden Mile." With ancient grapevines twisting around the pergola-topped patio and views overlooking rows of vineyard, you might swear you were in Italy. But, even better, you are in the Okanagan.

Jenna Pillon joined the Terrafina team in 2014. She became a culinary star fresh after graduating from Kelowna's Okanagan College Culinary School by winning the Junior Chef of the Year at the National Junior Culinary Championships. Terrafina is a female-driven force; there is a lot of passion here.

Jenna is married to chef Brent Pillon (Hillside Bistro) and describes life at home: "Being married to a chef is fantastic! Not only does he cook for me, but also he understands our industry and what is expected from a chef, and supports me every step of the way. When you cook all day and night, it's usually the last thing you want to do when you get home. But when we do, it's great. We've worked in the same restaurant together, and so we know how to move around the kitchen without stepping on each other's toes. It's our form of dancing."

f /Terrafina-Restaurant 🐦 @terrafinaresto terrafinarestaurant.com

The Cheese Maker ✤ Gitta Pedersen
Poplar Grove Cheese, Penticton

Gitta Pedersen is originally from Denmark, where she had her first career as a pediatric nurse. Arriving in the Okanagan, she jumped into the farm life, building a hugely successful winery and then a cheesery, making her a celebrated pioneer in the Okanagan cheese-making world. She now tends her own vineyard (with her own hands), and has stepped into more of an overseer role at the cheese shop, enjoying her busy life as a farmer and a mom.

Gitta explains how it evolved: "As the wine industry and tourism in the valley grew, the desire to start a cheesery was born. Coming from Denmark where cheese production (and consumption) is fairly high, I have always been interested in learning the process of cheese making. My cheese facility remains very small, and the production is completely hands-on. We have continued to make the same four cheeses that we started out with, wanting to produce quality cheeses that our customers and chefs will recognize and enjoy over the years. We like to keep things relatively simple! Also, in keeping it small, we continue to enjoy the benefits of a 'family' operation, where my 'cheese girls' are essential to the quality of our production."

Wine and cheese make an obvious perfect pairing, so Gitta went into business with her long-time friend Ross Hackworth of nearby Nichol Vineyard. He and partner Matthew Sherlock make Lock & Worth Wines with the grapes from Gitta's vineyard, and she sells them with her cheese in the wine & cheese shop on the farm. Along with artisan cheese and wine, this special shop offers a one-of-a-kind view over Naramata onto sparkling Okanagan Lake.

Gitta has added picnic tables so her guests can linger over lunch with a glass of Lock & Worth wine in one hand and a cracker slathered with luxurious cheese in the other—and linger they do.

f /poplar.grovecheese poplargrovecheese.ca

ROB SUMMERS

The Winemaker ❖ Rob Summers
Hester Creek Estate Winery, Oliver

Curt Garland purchased the beautiful Hester Creek Estate Winery in 2004. Two years later he brought on winemaker Rob Summers, who has created a rich wine portfolio that has celebrated much success. The winery property offers luxurious villas for rent and the Terrafina restaurant, where guests can while away hours surrounded by vineyards under the Oliver sun.

This 22,000 square-foot winery holds a bit of magic itself, it is actually built into the mountainside. A unique and totally eco-friendly building, the bunker-style design aims to leave a "smaller footprint" on the native topography. Veteran winemaker Summers says, "The terroir on the Golden Mile allows grapes to express true varietal character, with intensity and crisp, vibrant flavours. It really allows the characteristics of the grapes to shine through." The winery offers food and wine experiences, including tours, tastings, and cooking classes.

f /hestercreek 🐦 @hestercreek hestercreek.com

Apple Cake On Wheels

🍐 KLEMENS KOESTER

🏠 BC TREE FRUITS CO-OP

🍎 NIK & KATE DURISEK

This is going to become your "go-to" cake recipe from now on. It's so delicious and so versatile. Klemens Koester of Bread on Wheels in Kelowna says you can use any Okanagan fruit you wish. Okanagan plums, pears, apricots, peaches, or berries—all would be superb. This cake is so straightforward to make that you can invite your friend over for coffee and have it coming out of the oven in just over an hour. It's so fast—like a cake on wheels.

Makes 2 10-inch (25-cm) cakes or 1 large cake

Enjoy with Howling Moon Cidre Blanco

Dry and not sweet, with those tiny bubbles tickling your nose, it makes for a perfect food pairing and will make brunch, dessert or a snack feel like more of a celebration.

Preheat oven to 375°F (190°C). Grease and flour (your choice of) baking pans (dust pans with flour and shake out any excess to easily pop baked cakes out). In a mixer bowl, whisk butter and sugar together until nice and fluffy, then add eggs slowly and mix well. Add flour, baking powder, vanilla, and lemon zest. Mix until batter is even.

Spoon batter into cake pans evenly. Spread out until top is nice and smooth. Lay apple slices gently onto batter. Do not push into the batter.

Bake in the middle of the oven until golden brown, for approximately 30–40 minutes. Remove from oven and cool in the pan.

The nicest way to finish up: dust icing sugar over cake and glaze apples with hot apricot jam or jelly.

1 cup (250 mL) butter

1 cup (250 mL) granulated sugar

5 eggs

1½ cups (375 mL) all-purpose flour

2 tsp (10 mL) baking powder

2 tsp (10 mL) vanilla

zest of ½ a lemon

3 apples, peeled, cored, and sliced into ⅛-inch (3-mm) wedges

apricot jam, for glazing

icing sugar, for dusting

KLEMENS KOESTER

The Baker ❖ Klemens Koester
Bread on Wheels, Kelowna

What a brilliant idea! How would you like fresh bread and other treats delivered directly to your door? Klemens Koester's Bread on Wheels does exactly that. Klemens's high-quality baking is a favourite for many local chefs and restaurants.

His bakeshop is located on his gorgeous farm up in the hills of South Kelowna. Klemens's plan to work from home all started with a wood-fire oven that he built himself from rocks he found on his property. He began baking for weddings and special events, and word of his baking spread like wildfire. Soon calls came in asking for orders. Thankfully, his business has grown to a level where he now employs drivers and bakers to help with the workload. Everything is made from scratch, and a business that started with an offering of five different loaves, has jumped to a repertoire of over 300 products.

Originally from Switzerland, Klemens began his training as a baker at age 15 when, he says, "I grew a passion for it." He originally wanted to go into farming, but at the time, cost of land in his homeland was inaccessible. When he and his wife, Regula, moved to Canada, they were able to realize the dream of a farm. Their fairytale-like property has horses, goats, layer hens, and happy ducks and geese splashing in a pond—all with a soaring view over the valley.

Klemens shops at the BC Tree Fruits store and loves that all of his fruit pies and fruit products are made with Okanagan fruit. Sign up for delivery today!

f bread-on-wheels-bakery   breadonwheels.ca

The Farm Co-op ❖ BC Tree Fruits
BC Tree Fruits

For me, the logo of BC Tree Fruits represents our family business. My parents and my grandparents, my great-grandparents, and those before were all farmers and orchardists and made their living from the soil. My Grandpa (John) Weisbeck and Opa (Lambert) Schell, neighbours in East Kelowna's orchard district, would have been early members of the co-op, delivering their apples and other fruits downtown to the packing house on Clement Avenue. Now, there are 580 grower families that make up the membership of the BC Tree Fruits Co-op, all funneling their hard work and pride through this symbol of farm community. In exchange, BC Tree Fruits packs, stores, transports, and markets their produce. They also offer an on-site store where the public can shop from a wide variety of local fruit, vegetables, and other artisanal products. New to the co-op is Broken Ladder Apple Cider, made from the apple culls discarded at the packinghouse. This concept represents the tremendous U-turn that communities are making, returning slowly to the world of old, one built around sustainability and recycling. This much-needed change represents an awakening in consumer responsibility and a response to world security issues. The village mentality returns, which

NIK & KATE DURISEK WITH CHILDREN AIDEN & ARIANA, AND CIDER DOG, DEXTER

MY GRANDPA, JOHN WEISBECK, ON HIS EAST KELOWNA APPLE ORCHARD
CIRCA 1946 WITH THREE OF HIS EIGHT CHILDREN: WILMA SCHELL,
JOHN WEISBECK JR., AND, ON HIS LAP, MARION SCHELL.

The Apple Cider Makers ✢ Nik & Kate Durisek
Howling Moon Craft Cider, Oliver

Nik and Kate Durisek packed up their life in Vancouver, including their adorable two children, Ariana and Aiden, and their trusty dog, Dexter, and moved to the Okanagan in 2012. Following their dream, they started a business growing apples and making cider. Kate says, "The sun-kissed orchards and vineyards, the rolling hills, the pristine lakes all beckoned us to leave our coastal lives and migrate to a slower pace, a smaller community, and a hotter climate. In 2012 we packed up our 100 potted heirloom apple trees and purchased a property to plant them at; we've been making our Howling Moon Craft Cider ever since. We LOVE cider! We care about our apples, we care about our growers, we tenderly nurture each batch of cider through fermentation until its matured to perfection, and then we lovingly hand bottle and label each individual bottle ourselves." Their new tasting room is opening in Oliver and is sure to be a huge success.

f /howlingmooncraftcider   🐦 @howlingcider   howlingmoon.ca

for me, was only a short renaissance period. My grandparents brought that lifestyle with them as immigrants after World War II, when they, for the fourth time in their lives, would rebuild a life again from nothing but the land.

It was Father Pandosy, a French Catholic priest, who was responsible for the birth of true orcharding in the Okanagan. In 1862, he developed the first, large-scale apple farm on his mission (the museum and original site are located on Benvoulin Road in Kelowna). Roslyne Buchanan delivers a wonderful snapshot of our fruit-growing industry in her essay on page 189.

f /bctree   🐦 @bctreefruits   bctree.com

Chef Bernard's "Twisted" Carrot Cake

 BERNARD CASAVANT

 BONNIE CASAVANT

 JIM FAULKNER

Chef Bernard Casavant of Okanagan College in Kelowna, or "Chef B" as he is affectionately known, is famous for his "twists" or deconstructed dishes. This magnificent collection of flavours is a celebration of his wife Bonnie's garden. Make as many or as few of his components as you like. Chef B always garnishes this dish with delicious local treats, like ricotta cheese crumble, Everything Green culinary flowers and microherbs, and fire-roasted peaches (he suggests trying them preserved in plain water). Try adding some organic cold-pressed pistachio oil to the microgreens salad.

Serves 4

Enjoy with 2012 Semillon, Mt. Boucherie Estate Winery

A fresh and crisp wine boasting lemony aromas and citrusy flavours combined with Granny Smith apple.

Preheat oven to 325°F (160°C). Grease a loaf pan or 9- × 9-inch (23 cm × 23 cm) pan and set aside. Sift all dry ingredients together in a large bowl. Combine the oil, eggs, and juice, add to the dry ingredients and fold in. Fold in the shredded carrots.

Pour batter into the greased pan and bake for 25–30 minutes, or until a toothpick inserted into the centre comes out clean. Cool completely. Keep at room temperature.

Place a fine mesh sieve over a bowl and set aside. Bring a saucepot of water to a boil, then reduce to simmer.

In a bowl that fits the pot, combine the lemon juice, lemon zest, tea, sugar, and honey, whisking to combine. Place the bowl on the pot and whisk continuously, ensuring that the bowl is not touching the water. Continue to cook until the mixture is very thick (coats the back of a spoon or registers 175°F [80°C]) about 10–12 minutes. Remove the mixture from the heat and pour through the reserved fine mesh strainer.

Stir slowly, allowing the mixture to cool slightly to 140°F (60°C).

Add the butter in one piece at a time, whisking until each piece melts completely. Cool, stirring occasionally to prevent a skin from forming. Place in the fridge until cold and firm. Cover.

Cream cheese: In a small saucepan combine the honey, lavender, and apple juice. Bring to a simmer then whisk to extract the lavender essence. Cool to room temperature to let the lavender steep. Strain the essence over the cream cheese and whip until light and creamy. Keep at room temperature until serving.

Continued on page 180

Carrot cake

1 cup (250 mL) + 2 tsp
  (10 mL) flour
pinch salt
1 tsp (5 mL) baking soda
¼ tsp (1 mL) baking powder
2 tsp (10 mL) cinnamon,
  ground
1 tsp (5 mL) cardamom, ground
1 tsp (5 mL) fennel seed,
  ground
¾ cup (190 mL) + 1 Tbsp
  (15 mL) cane sugar
¼ tsp (1 mL) ginger, ground
¼ cup (60 mL) canola oil
2 free range eggs
2 Tbsp (30 mL) fresh
  orange juice
1 cup (250 mL) carrots,
  shredded

Chamomile citrus curd

(Chef's note: Blood orange also
  makes a great curd!)
½ cup (125 mL) + 2 Tbsp
  (30 mL) fresh lemon juice
zest of 1 lemon
1 tsp (5 mL) organic
  chamomile tea
¼ cup (60 mL) cane sugar
3 Tbsp (45 mL) buckwheat
  honey
4 large free-range eggs
  (or try duck eggs!)
1 cup (250 mL) unsalted butter,
  cubed at room temperature

Continued from page 179

In a small saucepan combine the honey, lavender, and apple juice. Bring to a simmer then whisk to extract the lavender essence. Cool to room temperature to let the lavender steep. Strain the essence over the cream cheese and whip until light and creamy. Keep at room temperature until serving.

Barley: In a nonstick pan over medium-high heat, toast the barley until golden brown. Shake the pan frequently to prevent barley from scorching. Once golden brown, remove the pan from heat, add the sugar and spices, and continue shaking the pan to distribute the seasoning well. Squeeze the juice from the half orange, shaking the pan to distribute. Pour onto a plate to cool. In a small blender, pulse briefly, maintaining some texture. Keep at room temperature.

Salad: The secret to this salad is the crispness of the microgreens and the balance of the sweet and sour flavours. Experiment a little as the season goes on, adding the various kale, lettuce, and herbs as they start showing in the garden.

Combine greens and orange zest in bowl, and keep cold. At the last minute, add sugar and toss to mix very well. Place on the plate.

Lavender-infused whipped cream cheese

2 Tbsp (30 mL) honey

1 Tbsp (15 mL) dried lavender blossoms

1 Tbsp (15 mL) organic apple juice

½ cup (125 mL) cream cheese

Toasted "pressed barley"

½ cup (125 mL) pressed barley

1 Tbsp (15 mL) powdered sugar

pinch ground cinnamon

pinch all spice

½ orange, for juicing

Everything Green microgreens salad

½ cup (125 mL) per person organic microgreens, light delicate flavors

¼ tsp (1 mL) powdered sugar

Pinch orange zest (use a microplane)

BERNARD & BONNIE CASAVANT

The Chef ❖ Bernard Casavant
Okanagan Chefs Association/Okanagan College, Kelowna
Chef B: Bernard Casavant Consulting

Chef Bernard plays an integral role in the culinary community of the Okanagan and, among other accomplishments, is the current president of the Okanagan Chefs Association. He is the recipient of a Distinguished Alumni Award from Vancouver Island University in 2011, an awarded member of the Canadian Culinary Federation's Honour Society 2012, and a BC Restaurant Hall of Fame Inductee. He is also the culinary manager of the Okanagan College's Culinary & Pastry Arts program. Also a talented artist, Chef Bernard creates beautiful wood serving platters (see photo on page 178) and has been known to draw his dishes to instruct his staff on his vision.

Says Chef Bernard, "As president of the Okanagan Chefs Association, it is a pleasure to interact with our general membership from North to South Okanagan. Through our monthly dinner meetings, we present guest speakers who educate our association on the awesome products we have in the Okanagan and as well the rest of BC. Along with providing education to our membership, we are also committed to a wide variety of community events, supporting an incredible array of noteworthy charities. One of our newest initiatives, Chefs in Classrooms—Edible Education, is very exciting. We have developed a committee to teach various grade three students to plant, grow, and cook produce. It's rewarding to see approximately 200 children (and their parents!) engaged and understanding how to grow their plants from seed. We're proud to be part of our community."

Chef B is also very proud of his wife, Bonnie, and her amazing garden. He explains, "For this dessert plate, it is a pleasure to focus on the incredible produce that my wife, Bonnie, produces. I find that with the right balance, this carrot cake and microgreens salad offers an interesting conclusion to a casual dinner party. The tartness of the curd paired with the spice of the carrot cake adds to the clean flavour of the micro greens."

The Farmer ✣ Bonnie Casavant
Everything Green, Kelowna

Bonnie Casavant's green thumb has taken her from landscaping to providing organic produce for Kelowna's finest restaurants. Gardening seems to be a passion that has been passed down through the generations of her family, and continues on through the hands of her own two children. Says Bonnie, "My memories of gardening go back to puttering in the garden with my grandpa when I was about eight years old. He was an avid gardener and won many awards, primarily for his flowers. Growing up, I helped my parents in their vegetable and flower garden, but my love for gardening and landscaping really took off when I was about 25, when I wanted to get our children interested in growing what they eat. It seems to have worked; our son, Kristopher, who lives in Los Angeles, has devoted his entire backyard to feeding his family. Our daughter, Steffanie, currently lives in Northern Alberta, which doesn't have much of a growing season, but she grows whatever she can in pots and planters. Both Kristopher and Steffanie involve their wee sons in their own gardens."

Bonnie explains, "My philosophy for gardening is simple—to be absolutely and totally organic. There is nothing that tastes better than eating a 'just-harvested' organic carrot, pea, or tomato. My goal is to convince every client to start a compost and discontinue using chemical fertilizers. I love being outdoors; I tell everyone the outside is my office!" She is inspired by the gardening practices of Paul Kaiser, who owns and operates Singing Frogs Farm in California, saying that she has "adopted his ideals for my garden. He believes we should treat the soil with respect, and mimic Mother

LEFT TO RIGHT: NIRMAL, PINKI & KAL GIDDA, JIM FAULKNER

Nature as best as we can. Next years' plans are to plant a few more varieties of tomato plants, try growing quinoa, and implement companion planting."

The Winemaker ✣ Jim Faulkner
Mt. Boucherie Family Estate Winery, Kelowna

The Gidda family has been growing grapes since 1968 and is the owner of approximately 300 acres of vineyard properties. As the winemaker for Mt. Boucherie, Jim Faulkner has the opportunity to make his wines from 100 percent estate-grown grapes coming from all across the Okanagan and Similkameen Valleys. Grapes are harvested from the Gidda's properties in Cawston, Okanagan Falls, Oliver, and the headquarters in West Kelowna where the Mt. Boucherie Estate Winery is located. The range of terroir that Jim has to create wines with is vast, and allows him a great diversity in the portfolio of wines produced, including 21 reds, whites, and ice wines.

Gingerbread Affogato

GIOVANNI (GIO) LAURETTA

KALAYRA ANGELYYS

An *affogato* is a coffee-based dessert or an amazing indulgence any time of day. I order them from Gio Lauretta at Giobean Espresso in Kelowna in the summertime when he sells his gelato. An *affogato* usually takes the form of a scoop of vanilla gelato or ice cream topped with a shot of hot espresso. At Gio's I usually get hazelnut gelato . . . Yum! So, for those of you who can make espresso at home, this is going to become your favourite, easy dessert for guests. Any of Ice Cream Artisan Kalayra Angelyys's amazing gourmet ice cream flavours would work, but this gingerbread flavour is perfect during the holiday season!

Makes 1

Pour hot espresso over the ice cream in a cup or bowl. Enjoy the hot and cold sensation as the ice cream melts into an "oh my God" kind of coffee milkshake.

Double shot of Giobean espresso

Scoop of Ice Cream Artisan Gingerbread ice cream

The Coffee Maker ❖ Giovanni Lauretta
Giobean Espresso, Kelowna

GIO LAURETTA

Giobean hit the Kelowna food scene in 2010 like a much-needed shot of espresso, bringing that unmistakable passion that comes from an authentic Italian coffee house. Breathing life into the cultural district of the city, it was an instant success.

Giobean not only provides outstanding, addictive java to the coffee aficionados in town, it also provides that sense of home and community. There is something so special about being greeted by a barista who remembers your name. Gio Lauretta and his wife, Lucy, have created a warm hub at the city's core, literally becoming a boardroom where people host meetings with friends and business associates alike. Daughter Claudia also works alongside her parents, learning the family trade with gusto.

Says Gio, "As my *nonno* [grandfather] said to me as a small boy growing up in Italy, 'Coffee should be as strong as a lion, as dark as night, but as sweet as love.'" The Giobean experience is a testament to Gio's Italian background and many years of experience in the coffee industry.

How did they get from Italy to Kelowna? Gio explains, "We'd been living in the UK 12 years after living in Italy, where we met. Then, on a vacation to Canada in June 2002, we were passing through British Columbia on our way to Vancouver from Revelstoke. We couldn't make it to Vancouver in an afternoon so we stopped in Kelowna for the night. By the time we left the next morning we knew this was the place we wanted to live. The feel of the place and the beauty of the surrounding area blew us away, and we decided Kelowna would be a great place to call home. It was a dream, and we were determined to hold onto our dream and not let it go. This dream came true as we landed in Kelowna in August 2009 with our two children, four suitcases, a business plan, and a lot of hope and determination to succeed. We knew pretty early on that our decision was the right one, and now six years on we can't imagine living anywhere else!"

f /giobean-coffee-the-italian-way 🐦 @giobean giobeancoffee.com

The Ice Cream Maker ❖ Kalayra Angelyys
Ice Cream Artisan, Kelowna

Kalayra Angelyys is the woman behind Ice Cream Artisan, the company creating this addictive indulgence, and she also offers catering services. What makes her gourmet ice cream and sorbet so special is that it is frozen instantly using liquid nitrogen, which allows all of the flavour and an ultra-rich, creamy texture to be retained. What I also love is that she uses all of the best ingredients, omitting the additives, preservatives, stabilizers, and emulsifiers that you will see in most other ice creams. This ice cream is essentially created from scratch and Kalayra sources her ingredients locally whenever possible.

And then there is the entertainment factor. Liquid nitrogen is added to the base ingredients in the bowl of her Kitchen Aid mixer creating a super fun smoke show! Kalayra explains, "As a gas, nitrogen is completely harmless. In fact, nearly 80 percent of the air you're breathing right now is made of nitrogen. And if you've ever eaten a steak, an omelette, or even a handful of trail mix, you've consumed nitrogen as part of your diet."

What an original idea to book an ice cream caterer for your corporate mixer, private party, birthday, wedding, reception, fundraising event, or festival. She makes a huge variety of flavours, including wine and beer, offers a dairy-free option, and can customize as well.

f /icecreamartisan 🐦 @icecreamartisan icecreamartisan.ca

KALAYRA ANGELYYS

History of Farms and Vineyards

Orchards, vineyards, and farmlands draped along lakesides, across valleys, and up hillsides are central to our Okanagan lifestyle. Yet, it was just 1811 that the first European, Scottish fur trader David Stuart (Pacific Fur Company), arrived. His trail lured his cousin, John Stuart (Hudson's Bay Company), more fur traders, and miners to a region home to Aboriginal people with strong traditions around food gathering, fishing, and hunting of indigenous species. As missionaries built the first non-native settlements at the head of Okanagan Lake about 1840 and Kelowna in 1859, the mission's religious, social, and cultural practices initiated change.

Apple trees were first planted by Hiram "Okanagan" Smith near Osoyoos around 1857 and by Father Pandosy at the French Catholic mission near Kelowna in 1862. To produce sacramental wines, Father Pandosy planted Okanagan's inaugural grapevines. Other settlers focused on cattle ranching and growing grain or tobacco while planting fruit trees for personal use.

The first step toward pioneering Okanagan fruit farming was when Lord John Aberdeen purchased the McDougall Ranch near the Okanagan Mission in 1890, renaming it Guisachan. Then, in 1891, he bought and moved to the Coldstream Ranch. On the properties, 100-acre orchards were planted including apples, crabapples, apricots, peaches, prunes, cherries, plums, raspberries, and strawberries. Appointed Governor General of Canada from 1893 to 1898, he built a Vernon jam factory and grew the Coldstream Ranch into one of the British Empire's largest fruit producers. Taking Aberdeen's lead, commercial growers planted large orchards while ranchers and farmers added smaller orchards, and by 1900, one million fruit trees supported the burgeoning industry.

After the gold mine venture that brought him to the Okanagan failed, John Robinson recognized fruit's potential and sold land to prospects in an area he called Peachland, and later in Summerland and Naramata. In 1910, the Kettle Valley Railway named Penticton as headquarters and this new rail broadened the Okanagan fruit industry's reach.

Such visionaries and developments, and the introduction of irrigation, fruit cooperatives, and research planted the seeds of innovation embedded in the Okanagan. It is this pioneering spirit that sustains today's farms and enabled the exponential growth of the wine industry.

ROSLYNE BUCHANAN

Farm & Winery

Bench 1775 Blissful Mojito

 VAL TAIT

Everything about Bench 1775 Winery on the beautiful Naramata Bench screams summertime and fun—from the to-die-for patio to its delicious wines, amazing events, and sparkling winemaker, Val, who also knows how to shake up a cocktail. This mojito pairs perfectly with summer!

Makes 4

Place ice in shaker, add rum, 8 mint sprigs, lime juice and Bliss icewine. Shake well and serve over ice in a highball glass. Top off each glass with a splash of club soda and garnish with a slice of lime and a sprig of mint. Raise your glass high and toast the blissful, lazy, delicious days of summer!

1 cup of ice

6 oz white rum

12 mint sprigs, or spearmint, 8 roughly torn into pieces

6 Tbsp (180 mL) fresh lime juice

1 oz Bench 1775 Bliss Icewine

Club soda

4 slices lime

The Winemaker ✤ Val Tait
Bench 1775 Winery, Naramata

Perched exquisitely on a vineyard-scape on the Naramata Bench, Bench 1775 has been called 'The Best Patio in the World' by wine writer Anthony Gismondi. And he isn't exaggerating.

Val Tait sparkles with the energy of someone truly in their element. Her studies included plant biochemistry and molecular genetics before she went on to viticulture and oeneology at UC Davis, which gives her complete insight into her wines from vine to glass. The stunning property and winery at Bench 1775 offer her an opportunity to share both her passion for winemaking and for celebrating the lifestyle in wine country. 'Fun' is a word she uses frequently when describing the spirit of the events planned at Bench 1775.

As for the new vintage white wines, they are an extension of Val and the Bench 1775 brand. Lively, full of bright flavours and Okanagan fruits, and so very easy to drink, they are a celebration of summer in a glass. And, as Val says, she loves to be able to enjoy one glass after another, so her technique of combining white grapes picked earlier (for their bright, green flavours) with the same fruit picked at a later date (for their ripe, sweeter flavours), blend together to provide the perfect balance of zestiness with a round finish.

f /bench1775   🐦 @bench1775   bench1775.com

VAL TAIT WITH LULU THE WONDER PUG

The Legendary Green Man Lavender Martini

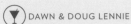

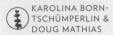

DAWN & DOUG LENNIE

KAROLINA BORN-TSCHÜMPERLIN & DOUG MATHIAS

Want to wow your guests? This beautiful, aromatic cocktail is a wonderful way to toast *la bonne vie*, Naramata style. This group of friends from the beautiful wine (& spirits) region of Naramata—Dawn and Doug Lennie of Legend Distilling and Karolina Born-Tschümperlin and Doug Mathias of Forest Green Man Lavender Farm—got together and made some magic with their artisanal products. Cheers!

Makes 1

Pour all ingredients into a cocktail shaker and shake well.

    Strain into a well chilled martini glass (keep those in the freezer, too).

    Garnish with lavender sprig. *Ooh la la!*

*We recommend keeping your gin in the freezer at all times so you don't have to mix your drinks with ice.

2 oz (60 mL) Legend Distilling Doctor's Orders Gin*

½ ounce (15 mL) dry vermouth

½ ounce (15 mL) Forest Green Man lavender simple syrup

1 Tbsp (15 mL) fresh lemon juice

1 small sprig lavender, for garnish

The Spirit Makers ✤ **Dawn & Doug Lennie**

Legend Distilling, Naramata

This hot new spirits distillery on the Naramata Bench appeared in 2014, just as the BC spirit and cocktail scene skyrocketed. Legend Distilling combines local ingredients to make handcrafted, small-batch gin and vodka, infused with local ingredients like sour cherry, rhubarb, and apricot, and a local-coffee-infused schnapps called Blasted Brew.

This style reflects their personal brand, too—owners Dawn and Doug Lennie are all about protecting their good earth and community. They recycle their mash by sharing it with farmer friends as fertilizer, and further support their community by using local ingredients, as demonstrated in their partnership with friends and neighbours Karolina Born-Tschümperlin and Doug Mathias at Forest Green Man Lavender, with whom they co-conspired to make their new bitters line.

The beautiful tasting room, built by Doug, offers windowed views to the rolling lawn below. The patio has a killer view onto Okanagan Lake, and visitors can have a tasting at the bar and/or order cocktails and tapas at The Legend Lounge. And you can book this gorgeous place for a private event or wedding. Make sure to prepare yourself for some shopping as well as the in-store cocktail accessories, local art, and goodies are fantastic!

f /legendnaramata   🐦 @legendnaramata   legenddistilling.com

The Farmers ✤ **Karolina Born-Tschümperlin & Doug Mathias**

Forest Green Man Lavender Farm, Naramata

Naramata Centre is one of the Okanagan's most beautiful landscapes and offers a respite from the busy wine world buzzing on the Bench above. This sleepy village is also the home to Forest Green Man Lavender Farm—very apropos since lavender has been used for centuries as a relaxing tonic to soothe the soul and the nerves.

Proprietors Doug Mathias and Karolina Born-

LEFT TO RIGHT: DOUG MATHIAS, KAROLINA BORN TSCHÜMPERLIN, DAWN & DOUG LENNIE

Tschümperlin are an absolute joy to meet; they are interesting, intelligent, fun, creative, and musical (they both play numerous instruments and have formed a local band), and they graciously welcome guests onto their farm. Together they create over 30 products for sale in their farm shop. Karolina is also a beautiful painter and her artwork is available to view and purchase in their new art gallery upstairs.

Karolina explains her vision of the farm: "Based on my farm experiences when I was growing up in Switzerland, we have tried to recreate a little bit of that experience with Forest Green Man. People can come and browse the farm, the lavender fields, and our fruit tree orchards, and then stay and sit down in the shade and enjoy some homemade lavender lemonade. They are welcome to watch us go about our various jobs of harvesting, drying, and essential oil distillation."

There are also two adorable cottages on the property available as vacation rentals, which are nestled among the fruit trees and gardens.

f /forest-green-man-lavender   forestgreenman.com, karolinaborn.com

Donna's Little Creek Gardens Greek Salad

DONNA DENISON

DALE ZIECH

DONNA DENISON

A bowl full of unabashed flavours featuring Okanagan vegetables and topped with one of Little Creek Dressing's incredible salad dressings. The recipe is one of dressing creator, Donna Denison's personal faves!

Serves 2

Combine all ingredients into a large salad bowl and toss with dressing.

Half organic red, orange, and
  yellow bell pepper, chopped
¼ cup (60 mL) organic
  red onion, chopped
2 small English cucumbers,
  diced
½ cup (125 mL) organic
  black olives, sliced
1 organic rainbow carrot, sliced
¼ cup (60 mL) organic roasted
  unsalted sunflower seeds
¼ cup (60 mL) organic
  dried cranberries
¼ cup (60 mL) organic
  feta cheese
⅓ cup (75 mL) organic
  garbanzo beans,
  rinsed and drained
2 Tbsp (30 mL) Little Creek
  Dressing's Cherry Balsamic

The Salad Dressing Maker ❖ Donna Denison
Little Creek Dressing, Kelowna

Little Creek Dressing is truly an Okanagan success story and pioneer in the local artisanal food-production world. Creator Donna Denison is a well-loved member of our food and farm community, and continues to enhance vegetables with the organic salad dressings born from her beautiful organic farm in West Kelowna.

The property has been in the Denison family for 70 years and has played host to many memorable events. Her flower gardens are as wonderful as the vegetable gardens, featuring roses galore and treasured plants and trees passed down to her through family. She and her husband, Dale Ziech, basically homesteaded this special farm and built the house themselves. He a musician and she a potter and artist, they raised a son and twin daughters, who all received the gift of creativity from their parents. Dale is renowned in the farm world as one of the original farmers to grow organic mixed greens and special vegetables for chefs at the beginning of the local food movement.

Donna says, "Dale had a realization that along with air and water, food gives us life, and he wanted to be sure to know how to grow his own food so he could feed himself and others." Little Creek Dressing now offers more varieties alongside its out-of-this-world Original (the best-bottled salad dressing ever): Spicy Strawberry, Cherry Balsamic, Okanagan Caesar, and Asian Apricot. If you ever have the luck to meet Donna, you will love her dressings even more. She sparkles with love and light and everything nice, and her dressings are infused with her magic.

f /littlecreek.dressing   littlecreekdressing.com

DALE ZIECH & DONNA DENISON

Blackberry Gazpacho with Cumin Cashew Crème & Bee Pollen

 JUDIE BARTA

 JUDIE BARTA

 JUDIE BARTA

JUDIE BARTA

Seasonal, local, and raw, this unique and delicious chilled soup by Judie Barta of Meadow Vista Honey Wines is so super healthy, it will leave you with a feeling of wellness.

Serves 4–6

Enjoy with Meadow Vista Cloud Horse Honey Wine

A dry, crisp traditional style, Cloud Horse uses only honey from a
single flower source to make this award-winning honey wine.

To make Cumin Cashew Crème: Soak the cashews for at least four hours. Drain the soaking liquid from the cashews and place in a blender. Add the cumin and salt, plus 1 cup (250 mL) fresh water. Blend until creamy, kind of like whipped cream. Store in a bowl with sealed lid until ready for soup.

To make Gazpacho: Add all of the ingredients to the blender and blend until desired consistency (Judie likes it a little chunky). Pour into individual bowls, garnish with a swirl of Cumin Cashew Crème, and sprinkle with bee pollen.

Cumin cashew crème

1 cup (250 mL) raw cashews

1 cup (250 mL) pure water

1 tsp (5 mL) cumin powder
   (or mortar and pestle the
   equivalent of seeds)

½ tsp (2.5 mL) Baltic sea salt

Blackberry gazpacho

4 cups (1 L) blackberries

1 cup (250 mL) cucumber,
   diced

½ jalapeno, seeded and diced

1 cup (250 mL) Cloud Horse or
   other off dry white wine

½ cup (125 mL) Meadow
   Vista honey

bee pollen

The Cook/Farmer/Beekeeper/Winemaker ❖ Judie Barta
Meadow Vista Artisan Farm Winery, Kelowna

A cook, farmer, beekeeper, and winemaker, Judie is also mom to two girls, is beautiful, and has a big heart that yearns to protect our planet.

Not a fan of mead or honey wine? This is the gal that is going to change your mind. Meadow Vista Honey Wines has won multiple awards for its sophisticated flavours and finessed palate. Barta's Bliss bubbly is a favourite, is made with honey and organic cherries, and is pink and delicious. Meadow Vista Honey Wines has evolved over the years, changing locations and branding, to become an artisan farm concept/winery.

Now with five beautiful acres and a tasting room/winery in agriculturally rich southeast Kelowna, Judie (the Queen Bee) is thriving. In addition to creating her award-winning honey wines, her farm includes organic blackberries and strawberries, as well as a spring crop of much-needed local organic asparagus. And—of course!—she also makes honey. The farm's attributes made her the perfect candidate to host Farm Folk/City Folk's annual Feast of Fields in 2015.

Judie's dream to combine wellness with food and wine is finally becoming a reality. Also a trained massage therapist and wellness expert, Judie still maintains a small clientele on the new farm as well as adding yoga classes. The culinary aspect of the farm is also evolving and she hosts events on the property. From an educational aspect, the farm represents a learning centre for promoting the survival of the honeybee and sharing the many wonderful healing properties of honey. Judie explains with a huge smile, "the farm has so much to offer,"—as does she!

f /MeadowVista 🐦 @HoneyWines meadowvista.ca

Forbes Farm Stuffed Turk's Turban Squash

The turban squash, also known as "Turk's turban" or "French turban," is a type of winter squash. It is an heirloom, predating 1820, and it really does look like a turban. Brothers Steve and Gordon Forbes own and operate their organic family farm in Oliver and are star producers at the local farmers' markets. All of their products are of the highest quality due to the passion of this hardworking family. The brothers are lovingly continuing the precedent set by their parents, Don and Jean Forbes, who purchased the farm in 1974.

Serves 4–6

Preheat the oven to 350°F (180°C). Cut off the top of the squash (like a jack-o'-lantern) and then remove seeds and pulp and discard. Mix all of the ingredients together except for the butter and half of the coconut sugar and then stuff the squash. Cover with the top of the squash and put onto a baking sheet. Melt the butter and pour on top and sprinkle small amount of coconut sugar. Bake for about 1½ hours, or until squash is fork-tender.

1 Turk's turban squash or similar good stuffing squash

1–2 diced apples

½ cup (125 mL) dried cherries or raisins

½ cup (125 mL) chopped nuts (almonds, hazelnuts or walnuts)

¼ cup (60 mL) coconut sugar, divided

¼ cup (60 mL) maple syrup

¼ cup (60 mL) coconut oil

1 tsp (5 mL) each of cinnamon nutmeg and cardamom

¼ cup (60 mL) butter

STEVE FORBES

AVAILABLE TODAY!

ME

TOMATO

BASIL

EGGPLANT

GARLIC

CUKES

Upper Bench Spot Prawns & Paneer

SHANA MILLER

GAVIN MILLER

This recipe by Shana Miller of the Upper Bench Winery & Creamery is easy, delicious, and versatile. You can use ricotta in place of the paneer, and substitute wild prawns for spot prawns. If the spots are in season, though, use them. They are a locally sourced West Coast treasure and can be found fresh from the ocean at Codfathers Seafood (in Kelowna) when in season, or frozen.

Serves 2

Enjoy with 2013 Riesling, Upper Bench Winery

This delicious Riesling offers notes of lime, honey, and pear on the nose, followed by flavours of Okanagan apples, stone fruits with a zing of bright, refreshing acidity.

Heat half of the oil in a cast iron frying pan and lightly pan-fry the paneer (one minute per side), remove, and set aside. Add the remaining oil; add garlic and shallot, and sauté until soft. Add the diced tomatoes and cook until the sauce thickens (10–15 minutes). Add prawns and cook for another 2 minutes. Add the paneer and heat thoroughly. Plate up and sprinkle with parsley. Simply rip off a piece of baguette and dip in sauce.

Paneer is a fresh, unsalted white cheese popular in Indian cuisine. It requires no ageing or culturing, and is very easy to make at home, so give it a go!

To make it from scratch: Sterilize all equipment being used. Pour milk into a large stainless steel pot and slowly heat milk to boiling at 212°F (100°C), stirring gently so it doesn't burn. Be patient, it will be worth it. As milk begins to boil, quickly remove from heat.

Add lemon juice or vinegar and stir. You will see the curd separate from the whey

Let sit for a few minutes, pour through the cloth-lined colander. Gather the four corners of your cloth and twist to expel whey. Return cheese to the colander, sit colander over the pot, place a small plate on top of the cheese and weigh down (a tin of tomatoes work well). Let sit overnight.

2 Tbsp (30 mL) olive oil, divided

2 cloves garlic, minced

1 shallot, minced

3 Roma tomatoes, diced (diced and canned work too)

12 prawns

½ portion (1 cup) Paneer sliced ½-inch (1-cm) thick (store-bought or made from scratch, see recipe below)

1 Tbsp (15 mL) fresh parsley, chopped

salt & pepper

baguette, herbed or regular

1 gallon (4 L) whole milk (standard milk, NOT homogenized)

4 Tbsp (60 mL) freshly squeezed lemon juice or vinegar

Equipment

big spoon for stirring milk

large heavy-bottom stockpot

thermometer

cloth-lined colander/sieve

The Wine & Cheese Makers ❖ Gavin & Shana Miller
Upper Bench Winery & Creamery, Penticton

SHANA & GAVIN MILLER

Please allow me to introduce our wine and cheese makers: Gavin and Shana Miller. This couple—featured on our cover—represents not only the quintessential pairing of wine and cheese but also passion and commitment to excellence.

A combination of passions brought owners Gavin and Shana Miller together many years ago: he's a winemaker from the UK; she's a cheese maker from Nova Scotia. Now married 16 years, they long shared the dream of owning a business together.

That magical day arrived in 2010, when a vineyard on Penticton's Upper Bench came up for auction. Since the coupled opened the doors to Upper Bench Winery & Creamery, the Okanagan food and wine world has been buzzing with excitement. Gavin is a very well known and respected winemaker with a history of creating wines at some of our most celebrated Okanagan wineries. His Upper Bench Estate vineyard grows seven varietals on seven acres. The vines are hand-tended and meticulously farmed without the use of chemicals or pesticides. Gavin is a *vigneron*, meaning he both grows the grapes and makes the wine.

Gavin and Shana have created a European-style farm gate destination where visitors can pop in to purchase wine and cheese. In the summer months, the pergola-topped patio next to the wine shop provides a perfect oasis to recharge while on your food and wine trail in Naramata. A perfect glass of wine paired with the perfect cheese and enjoyed al fresco in the vineyard is what wine country is all about.

The Miller's also offer the country's only Curds & Corks Club—wine and cheese pairings delivered to your door. What could be better?

f /upperbench 🐦 @upperbench upperbench.ca

Roche Basque Cod & Chorizo Stew

PÉNÉLOPE ROCHE

PÉNÉLOPE & DYLAN ROCHE

Pénélope Roche's family is from the Basque region of France where mild fish and spicy sausage are a favourite flavour pairing. Pénélope, co-founder of Roche Wines in Penticton, not only has a passion for wine making but a passion for cooking too. She loves to cook with the flavours of her native France. *Piment d'Espelette* is a renowned Basque spice, but is not available here, unfortunately. Pénélope suggests hot smoked paprika, chili flakes, or even chipotle powder as a replacement.

Serves 6–8

Enjoy with 2013 Pinot Gris, Roche Wines

Asian pear, ginger spice, and floral overtones introduce this typical Pinot Gris.
The wine opens with aeration and swells to a broad mid-palate rich with ripe pear
and lemon zest. Electric acidity carries the wine to an intense, long and focused finish.

Preheat oven to 400°F (200°C). In a Dutch oven (we love Le Creuset) melt half of the duck fat (or butter) and add chorizo. Cook until the chorizo browns and then take it off to drain on a paper towel. In the same Dutch oven, add the sliced onion and garlic. Cook until the onion becomes transparent then add parsley and the *piment d'Espelette* (or substitute). Stir until all is combined well. Add beans with their juice and season with salt and pepper. Add bouillon if you prefer a more liquid consistency.

Stir well and then take off the heat and add breadcrumbs on top of your dish.

Place your Dutch oven in the oven and bake for 20 minutes. If breadcrumbs do not brown, turn on broil at the end until browned. While your beans are baking, add the leftover duck fat to a frying pan. Fry cod steaks on both sides until cooked. Both sides should be crunchy. Scoop a portion of beans onto serving plates and top with a cod steak. Sprinkle with parsley and piment d'Espelette. *Et voila!*

1 Tbsp (15 mL) duck fat (or butter), divided

2 small chorizo sausages, sliced thickly (mild or spicy, keep in mind the piment d'Espelette is hot)

1 onion, cut in thin slices

4 cloves garlic, finely chopped

2–3 Tbsp (30–45 mL) parsley, chopped

1 tsp (5 mL) piment d'Espelette (or hot smoked paprika)

1 28-oz can of white beans

salt & pepper

vegetable or chicken bouillon

3 Tbsp (45 ml) panko or coarse breadcrumbs

8 cod steaks

parsley and piment d'Espelette, for garnish

EUGENE, DYLAN, PENELOPE, & EILEEN ROCHE

The Winemakers ❖ Pénélope & Dylan Roche
Roche Wines, Penticton

What could be more romantic than two winemakers falling in love? He is from North Vancouver, she is from Bordeaux, and both are classically trained winemakers. The two met in New Zealand, over a tank full of grapes. Pénélope Roche recalls, "I met Dylan in 2005 in Hawke's Bay in New Zealand. After my studies in Bordeaux I travelled to make wine in different countries (Spain, Australia); my goal was to make two vintages in one year (in both the southern and northern hemispheres). Dylan had the same idea, and he was coming from Burgundy where he completed his winemaking studies. I was working for a small family winery and he came by one day to drop off a mutual friend. I was head to toe in a tank full of grapes, but I heard him speaking French—and the rest is history!"

Pénélope hails from a centuries-old, legendary wine family in Bordeaux—château Les Carmes Haut-Brion. The château has an amazing history: "Taken over by the state during the French Revolution, Les Carmes Haut-Brion was sold in 1840 to Léon Colin, a Bordeaux wine merchant and ancestor of the Chantecailles. The Chantecaille-Furt family owned and managed the estate for generations, until quite recently," Pénélope explains. "When my family sold the family estate château Les Carmes Haut-Brion at the end of 2010 it was a big change for us. I was in charge of the winemaking, the vine growing, and sales and marketing, and Dylan was working at a winery in Margaux. After some time to think, the decision to move here was clear. Dylan is from North Vancouver and he grew up coming to the Okanagan every summer to their family cabin on the lake in Carr's landing. We visited many times and loved the wine region, so we put everything in a container and moved to Penticton in May 2011. We both feel very happy to be here in the valley and trust it will grow to become a world-renowned wine destination. I want people in France to stop thinking, *Canada, oh yes, they just produce ice wine over there*. Our goal is to make people in Europe talk about us! Our valley has a very high potential to grow grapes and make some fabulous wine."

🐦 @rochewinery   rterrolr.ca

Hot Ross Apple Cider

Dave and Theressa Ross at the East Kelowna Cider Co. in Kelowna offer six unique hard ciders to choose from. Hot apple cider is always a delicious treat in the colder months in the Okanagan, and if it's local cider, it's even better. This drink brings back memories of Dave's dad, Dave Sr., pulling us around the snowy orchards as little kids in a train of sleighs behind his ski-doo.

Serves 4

In a saucepan, add the apple cider, cinnamon stick, cloves, maple syrup and nutmeg. Heat and gently simmer for 10–15 to infuse flavours (do not boil). Serve in mugs, with or without rum.

2 bottles Ross Soft Apple Cider

1 cinnamon stick

4 cloves

nutmeg, grated

2 Tbsp (30 mL) maple syrup

shot of rum (optional for grown-ups)

THERESSA & DAVE ROSS

The Farmers/Cider Makers ❖ Dave & Theressa Ross

East Kelowna Cider Company, Kelowna

The Ross family joins my family legacy of orchardists on beautiful East Kelowna Road. Dave and Theressa are continuing that family tradition, but adding a new spin by making cider from the apples. Their East Kelowna Cider Company was actually the first land-based cidery in BC, and offers seasonal farm tours. Ciders and other products are available for sale at the on-site tasting room. Dave and Theressa grow five varieties of peaches, nine varieties of apples, pears, plums, prunes, cherries, and apricots.

A little history about the Ross family: Charles (Grandpa) Ross purchased the orchard in 1942, the 20-acre orchard was planted with mainly apples and a small block of cherries. When Grandpa reached retirement each of his sons, David Albert and Kenneth Charles, bought 10 acres from him and changed the orchard planting to only apples. Dave Sr. married

DAVE ROSS SR. TAKING THE EAST KELOWNA NEIGHBOURHOOD
KIDS FOR A SLEIGH RIDE , CIRCA 1974

Edith Philpott and had three children in his father's family home. Today Dave Jr. and his wife Theressa own Ken's 10-acre piece and are managing the family homestead with their children. They also make logo-stenciled apples!

f /ekcider 🐦 @ekcider eastkelownacider.com

Oma's Prune Kuchen

This *kuchen* is Julianna Schell's (my oma) recipe and it rates a close second in the Schell family favourites recipe file (first will always be apple pie). I love the versatility and the size of this coffee cake cooked on a baking sheet. The trick of using vanilla sugar was a recent alteration to the recipe by my mom, Marion Schell.

Makes 12–16 pieces

Preheat oven to 350°F (180°C). Make topping by combining all dry ingredients and cutting in the cold butter with a pastry cutter until a coarse meal texture is achieved (you can also use your food processor to achieve this by pulsating the chop button). For batter, combine dry ingredients in a large bowl. Mix wet ingredients in another smaller bowl. Add wet ingredients to dry ingredients using wooden spoon and mix well. Pour into 10- × 15-inch (23 × 38 cm) high-rimmed baking sheet. Spread fruit over batter in a generous layer. Top with crumb mixture. Bake approximately 35–40 minutes until lightly browned. Refrigerate leftovers. Freezes well. This cake works well with other Okanagan fruits or berries like apricots, apples, cherries, or blueberries, so you can vary your cake by the season.

Topping

1 cup (250 mL) flour

½ cup (125 mL) sugar

1 pkg vanilla sugar (available locally at Illichmann's Meats, Sausages & Gourmet Foods)

½ cup (125 mL) cold butter

Batter

2 cups (500 mL) flour

3 tsp (15 mL) baking powder

1 tsp (5 mL) salt

1 cup (250 mL) sugar

2 eggs

⅔ cup (150 mL) vegetable oil

1 cup (250 mL) milk

2 tsp (10 mL) vanilla

½ tsp (2.5 mL) lemon juice

12 local Italian prune plums (long, purple, oval-shaped), washed, dried, pitted, quartered (or enough to make one layer on batter)

Granny's Apple Pie

P-I-E. Three letters that spell home. Lucky for me, I come from a family of orchardists and piemakers. Consequently, I am often still welcomed through the front door at home around harvest time with the sweet wafting aromas of apple pie. It's so delicious, that my brothers would not bother with cutting a mere slice when we were growing up—they would simply grab a fork, one pie each, and sit down to feast.

The secret, my mom says, is all in the crust. One must use lard and not shortening to achieve the ultimate flakiness. Regardless of that helpful tip, I know that the use of our own apples, grown on our orchard, is what makes mom's pies extra tasty—that, along with a good dose of love from the baker. My mom is known for making the best apple pies around, but she gives all the credit to her mother, my granny, Katherine Weisbeck, now 98 years old, and the original creator and pie queen.

Makes 1 pie

Mix dry ingredients together (first 4). Cut the lard into the dry ingredient mixture using a pastry cutter or two butter knives until it reaches a crumbly texture with pieces no larger than ¼ inch (6 mm).

Using a glass 1-cup (250-mL) measuring cup, add the egg and vinegar and beat with a fork. Fill the cup with water up to the 1-cup measurement line.

Add egg mixture to flour, mixing as little as possible (this keeps the crust flaky). Shape dough into 6–8 rounds, squeezing mixture tougher with your hands. On a floured board, roll each round to about ⅛-inch (3-mm) thick and place in a 9-inch (23 cm) pie shell. Trim dough around tin or pie plate, and then fill with apple filling.

Preheat oven to 350°F (180°C). Peel and core apples and then cut into slices, and then cut those in half. Load the apples into the pie shell on top of the crust until heaping (remember they will shrink considerably). Sprinkle with sugar and then generously with cinnamon. Dot around 6 pats of butter. Roll another pastry round out to make the top crust. Lie on top of apples and then trim around the tin or plate, leaving enough to pinch for decoration. Pinch around the edges to seal or use a fork to press into dough to seal. Using a pastry brush, brush egg wash over the top crust. Bake for 1 hour or until crust is golden brown. Remove to cool on rack. Pass out the forks!

Crust

5 cups (1.25 L)
   all-purpose flour
½ tsp (2.5 mL) baking powder
1 Tbsp (15 mL) salt
2 tsp (10 mL) brown sugar
1 lb (500 g) Tenderflake lard
1 egg
1 tsp (5 mL) vinegar
water

Apple filling (per pie)

Apples, probably 6–8 per pie,
   depending on size (any type
   will work, but McIntosh
   is the family favourite for
   flavour and the way it breaks
   down in the oven)
½ cup (125 mL) sugar
cinnamon
butter, in ½ tsp (2 mL)-sized
   pats
1 egg, beaten in a small bowl

Auntie Ruby's "Oh My" Pear Pie

There is a pie for almost every fruit or berry that we grow here in the Okanagan. Besides apple, I have another family favourite: my Auntie Ruby's Pear Pie! Perfect for the time of year when pears are at their peak, this unique treat would be a winner at any pie competition. Auntie Ruby (Leinemann) was a supermom with seven kids who spent much of her time in the kitchen creating delicious comfort food. We miss you, Auntie Ruby.

Serves 6–8

Preheat oven to 350°F (180°C). Place pears in a star shape in the pie shell. Sprinkle with cinnamon. Make custard. Beat 3 egg yolks, add milk, sugar, and vanilla and then beat flour in mixture. Pour custard over pears. Bake for one hour or until just set. Remove from oven to cool (make sure it is cool before adding meringue or it will melt).

Make meringue. Beat egg whites, vanilla, cream of tartar, and sugar until stiff peaks form. Top pie with meringue and bake for another 10 minutes, or until peaks are golden brown. Devour.

3 ripe Bartlett pears, cored
   & sliced in half
1 baked pie shell (store-bought
   or see my Granny's
   recipe, page 211)
1 tsp (5 mL) cinnamon
3 egg yolks (whites reserved
   for meringue)
¾ cup (175 mL) whole milk
1 cup (250 mL) sugar
1 tsp (5 mL) vanilla
1 heaping Tbsp (20 mL) flour
3 egg whites
½ tsp (2.5 mL) vanilla
¼ tsp (1 mL) cream of tartar
⅓ cup (75 mL) sugar

HILLARY SCHELL

Mom's Rhubarb Pie

Another family pie recipe! Rhubarb is one of those complicated vegetables that intrigues people, but no one knows quite what to do with. It's so pretty with its bright fuchsia and green stalks. As a child, I remember dipping the sour stalks into sugar to suck on (not recommended for modern kids!). This pie offers wonderful sweet and sour flavours, and a side of vanilla ice cream will take it to the next level. This the perfect springtime desert to celebrate the first growth in your garden.

Makes 1 pie

Preheat oven to 350°F (180°C). Pour hot water over rhubarb in a large bowl, stir in baking soda and let sit.

In mixer, beat together eggs, milk, flour, sugar and butter.

Drain rhubarb and add to mixer.

Fill unbaked pie shell (arrange lattice topping if using). Bake for 1½ hours on oven rack (bottom third). Place pie on a cookie sheet covered with tin foil to catch overflow drips.

Cool and enjoy!

4 cups (1 L) rhubarb

1 tsp (5 mL) baking soda

2 eggs

1 Tbsp (15 mL) milk

1½ cups (375 mL) sugar

⅓ cup (75 mL) flour

1 Tbsp (15 mL) butter, room temperature

1 unbaked 10-inch pie shell (can be made with top pastry layer or with lattice as shown in photo. To make from scratch use my Granny's pastry recipe, page 211)

Gatzke's Famous Peach Salsa

Against all odds, I have wrangled the recipe for Al Gatzke's Famous Peach Salsa, also available at the farm shop at Gatzke's Orchard in Oyama, made with the peaches grown on the farm. Enjoy!

Makes about 15 2-cup (500-mL) jars—enough for all your friends!

Chop all of the fruit and vegetables into small cubes. Mix the rest of the ingredients together, except for the cornstarch and brown sugar. Cook in a large pot, on low until the mixture comes to the boil. Boil gently for about 30 minutes, or until all of the ingredients are soft. If there is still a lot of juice in the pot, drain some off and then add the cornstarch/water mixture and stir until mixture thickens.

If sweetness is needed add ½ cup (125 mL) of brown sugar at a time until desired sweetness is reached. Fill sterilized jars and screw on lids. Process in a water bath for 17 minutes at a rolling boil.

16 cups (4 L) peaches, chopped
6 cups (1.5 L) onions, chopped
14 cups (3.5 L) peppers (your
   choice of colour), chopped
3 Tbsp (45 mL) garlic, minced
6 Jalapeno peppers, minced
⅓ cup (75 mL) white sugar
1½ cups (375 mL)
   white vinegar
½ cup (125 mL) lemon juice
¼ cup (60 mL) coarse salt
1 Tbsp (15 mL) dried oregano
2 Tbsp (30 mL) curry powder
1 Tbsp (15 mL) cumin
1 Tbsp (15 mL) cornstarch
   dissolved in ¼ cup
   (60 mL) of water
brown sugar to taste (optional)

The Farmer ❖ Al Gatzke

Gatzke's Orchards, Oyama

Gatzke's Orchards in Oyama is renowned for its amazing fruit and vegetable stand overlooking sparkling Wood Lake. The farm has evolved into an incredible venue for events, concerts, and even weddings. Al Gatzke, the man, the legend, is loved by all for his good nature and dedication to farming and celebrating the agricultural industry in our province. He is a proud farmer and prouder Oyamian who was born and raised on the land he farms on. He is carrying on the tradition of farming that his grandfather began on that land in 1929 and is now offering over 50 varieties of tree fruits throughout the season! With fruit and a wide array of vegetables, this is a destination fruit stand where visitors can tour the farm and see the fruits on the trees. They have a farm shop where they sell many delicious pies, preserves—including the peach salsa—and now a little eatery, The Orchard Café. Visitors can relax and enjoy the atmosphere of a working farm, which happens to have a beautiful view of Duck Lake. Al has recently taken his GO (Gatzke Orchard) Foodism dinners featuring local star chefs preparing dinners sourced from his farm, and serving them on the farm. They are a unique opportunity to really connect with the land and farm.

f /gatzke.orchards   🐦 @GatzkeOrchard   gatzkeorchard.com

AL GATZKE

Acknowledgments

Thank you to the incredible cast of people that participated in this book. The spirit and passion of each and every one of you inspires me.

Thank you to the farmers, orchardists, drink makers, artisans, foragers, chefs, butchers, bakers, and wine and cheese makers for your passion and commitment to making our world a more delicious, healthful place to be, and for taking the time to share your stories with me. Thank you for teaching us your Old World sustainability practices, reminding us to treasure the good earth we have been blessed with, and setting the table for the generations who will follow.

Thanks to Chef Rod Butters for organizing his fabulous team of chefs from RauDZ Regional Table to come to our home to cook the Sunday Night Supper. David McIlvride, thank you for photographing that delicious event and for your gracious photo consulting and support—you and Alison (Spatula Media) have been such stalwart advocates for our local industry and my own endeavours. Kevin Trowbridge, thank you for your photo tutorials and tech support!

Dona Sturmanis, thank you for your kind enthusiasm and encouragement. You were a brave heart, a wise teacher, and a champion for our community. You will be deeply missed but never forgotten.

Thank you to Team Touchwood! Taryn, Renée, Pete and Tori—what a pleasure to work with all of you. Thanks for making this book happen so quickly and for translating the power of this amazing community through the pages of this book.

Thanks to my wonderful family for your constant support, love and inspiration—I am truly blessed. To my special friends who have always been in my corner: I treasure you all.

And to my husband Mark: You are the best friend and partner I could ever ask for. Thank you.

Index

Photo credits
Cover image: David McIlvride, Spatula Media/ spatulamedia.ca
Page 20: Page Nystrom pancakes: Rae Campbell @raeligionfoto
Page 35: BX Cider Family: Jaime Lauren Photography
Page 53: Jennifer Cockrall-King photo: Curtis Trent Photography
Page 93: Covert Family Winery photo: Lionel Trudel/ trudelphoto.com
Page 98: Green Croft Gardens Organic Corn & Chantelle Pasta: CedarCreek Estate Winery
Page 119: Maverick Estate Winery: Lionel Trudel/trudelphoto.com
Page 130: Chef Brian Fowke: Hannes van der Merwe
Page 135: Culmina Winery: Lionel Trudel/trudelphoto.com
Page 146: RauDZ layout: David McIlvride, Spatula Media/ spatulamedia.ca
Page 161: La Frenz Winery: Lionel Trudel/trudelphoto.com
Page 165: Summerland Sweets, Ron Taylor: Stephanie Seaton/ Unlimited Vision
Page 183: Mt. Boucherie Winery family & winemaker: Lionel Trudel, trudelphoto.com
Page 187: Kalayra Angelyys: Emma Flegg
Page 196: Donna's Little Creek Gardens Greek Salad (food shot): Amber and Kerisa Denison